P9-BYS-062

food network kitchens

HOW TO BOIL WATER

life beyond takeout

Meredith® Books
Des Moines, Iowa

Copyright © 2006 by Meredith Coporation. All materials provided in this book by Television
Food Network, G.P., including all text, are owned by Television Food Network, G.P.
Copyright © 2006 by Television Food Network, G.P. All rights reserved. Food Network is a
service mark and/or registered trademark of Television Food Network, G.P. All photography
copyright © 2006 by Meredith Corporation and Television Food Network, G.P.

All rights reserved. No part of this book may be reproduced in any form
without written permission from the publisher.

Meredith Books
1716 Locust Street
Des Moines, Iowa 50309–3023
www.meredithbooks.com

First Edition.
Printed in the United States of America.
Library of Congress Control Number: 2006921257
ISBN-13: 978-0-696-22686-1
ISBN-10: 0-696-22686-3

Does "how to boil water" raise more questions than answers?

Then this book's for you.

We, Food Network Kitchens, asked you, our readers and viewers, what you wanted from an I-can't-cook-but-want-to-learn cookbook. You told us you wanted to feel comfortable and confident in the kitchen. You said you wanted real, honest food you could really make. You said dinner was takeout and breakfast was stressful.

Time to change that.

The recipes in this book are written for busy beginners. They pack big, global flavors; use supermarket ingredients; and range from Toast (page 19) to Thanksgiving (page 151). It's a completely doable repertoire of recipes you can rely on, no matter the audience or occasion. Picky palates, starving friends, weeknights, holidays—this book covers it all.

Good food comes from good recipes and good info. So we've packed the book with tips, shortcuts, and photos to help you succeed at everything from grocery shopping to pan-frying. We bring you tasty food, useful advice, and everything you need to transform your dining table from a temple of takeout to a desirable destination.

Learning to cook is all about basics, like how to hold a knife or peel an onion; cooking itself is about creativity and fun. Welcome to the best of both worlds.

(And for the record, put tap water in a pot, put the pot on a burner on the stove, cover the pot with a lid, and turn the burner to high. Wait. Big bubbles = boiling.)

who's who

Food Network Kitchens is the team behind the scenes at Food Network. We're the chefs, researchers, recipe developers, cooks, writers, and food stylists who work on the fabulous food you see on TV. And we also develop recipes, write cookbooks, and answer your questions online and in newspapers. We spend every day with food, whether it's cooking it, tasting it, writing about it, or researching it.

Left to right, starting from the top: Susan Stockton, Katherine Alford, Mory Thomas, Rupa Bhattacharya, Sarah Copeland, Jay Brooks, Rob Bleifer, Suki Hertz, Andrea Steinberg, Jacob Schiffman, Santos Loo, Vince Camillo, Dave Mechlowicz, Miriam Garron, Athen Fleming, Bob Hoebee

what's in this book

recipes

Lots of them. All especially designed for the beginner cook and meant to guide you through every step, from when to turn the oven on to how to serve the final dish.

ingredient list
Both what you need to make the dish and a quick shopping list.

instructions
Step-by-step details on how to prep, time, organize, and cook your food.

tips
Bits and pieces of helpful info, in one or more of these categories:

TIPS **shopsmart**
What to look for in ingredients and how to store them at home.

cook's note
Recipe-specific tips for cooking, serving, storing, and leftovers.

don't panic
Common errors and quick fixes.

a side of history
The backstory on a recipe— What's its deal? Where's it from?

wisdom
Get the benefit of FNK experience for ultimate results.

make it your own
Substitutions that work to expand your repertoire.

upgrades
Once you've mastered a recipe, take it to the next level.

pictures

Lots of those, too, intended both to explain and inspire. You'll find how-to pictures of everything you might want to know, whether it's how to hold and use a knife, how to roll out piecrust, or even just what a head of garlic looks like.

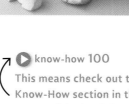

▶ know-how 100
This means check out the Know-How section in the center of the book (see pages 96-109) for pictures and instructions on techniques used in the recipe.

more

Chapters start with mini guides to get you on your feet and ready to go. And if you're wondering about things like meal planning, choosing wine, or having friends over for dinner, we've included that too.

table of contents

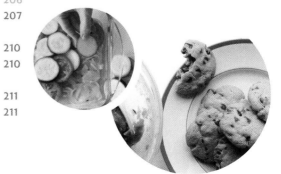

how to set up a kitchen

You don't need a lot of stuff to properly outfit a kitchen. What you want is tools that fit your style of cooking, how many people you cook for, and what kind of food you cook.

must-haves row 1: knives: chef's, serrated, paring; cutting board (or 2 to prevent cross-contamination); measuring cups: set for dry measuring from $\frac{1}{4}$ cup to 1 cup; measuring spoons: set from $\frac{1}{8}$ teaspoon to 1 teaspoon; spouted glass measuring cup (2-cup) row 2: 2 spoons, slotted and regular; wooden spoon; small metal spatula (i.e., pancake flipper and cookie remover); rubber spatula (heatproof is best); can opener; box grater; rasp (zester); peppermill row 3: peeler; whisk; tongs; instant-read thermometer; 1 set of microwave-safe nesting bowls, large to small row 4: medium saucepan with lid; small nonstick skillet; medium skillet with lid; dutch oven, medium or large

must-haves large pot for pasta with insert that doubles as colander and steamer; roasting pan with rack; glass baking dishes, 8x8-inch and 9x13-inch; salad spinner; broiler pan

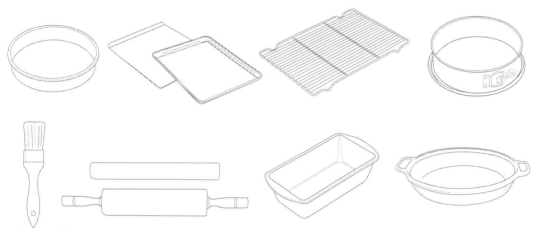

if you like to bake row 1: cake pan, 9-inch round; cookie sheet; rimmed baking sheet; cooling rack; springform pan row 2: pastry brush; rolling pin; metal loaf pan, 9x5x3-inch; glass pie pan

nice extras row 1: glass baking dish, 8x11-inch; casserole dish, 3-quart; colander; deep-frying thermometer; ladle row 2: cast-iron skillet; plastic containers with lids for leftovers; ridged cast-iron grill pan; immersion blender; blender; food processor

shopping & storage

Good food starts with good ingredients.
You can get those ingredients any number of
ways, whether it's regular express-lane trips,
big-box stores, the farmer's market, or once-
a-week grocery hauls. Whatever works for
you, here's how to make it easy:

think ahead

- Lists really work. Keep a list of staples (like paper towels and olive oil) on your computer or your fridge. Buy these items in bulk once a month so you can focus on the fresh stuff the rest of the time.

- For fresh foods, clean out the fridge before you make your list; you'll have a better idea of what you really need. Don't get stuck in a rut. Incorporate new recipes and ingredients into your shopping list.

- Plan seasonally, be flexible: Buy fruits and vegetables in season (check out pages 20 and 206 for tips on how). The better your ingredients, the less work you have to do to make them taste great. And stay open to inspiration. For example, if you planned on spinach but the escarole looks fantastic, buy the escarole.

- If you're a once-a-week shopper, plan to use perishable food (like fresh fish, berries, or salad greens) earlier in the week; save the hardy vegetables, citrus, or pantry items for later.

strategize

- In supermarkets, all the fresh food and perishables are usually located around the perimeter of the store. Shop from the back of the store to the front to speed up your trip and grab fruits and veggies at the very end so they don't get squished.

- Get the most for your money. The more that's been done to food (if it's prepared for you, like marinated meat or chopped veggies), the more it'll cost; you're paying for the convenience. The price of an ingredient, especially oils and vinegars, isn't necessarily related to the quality or taste—experiment and buy small bottles until you find out what you like.

- Farmers' markets are great—you can check out all kinds of not-sold-in-supermarkets fruits and veggies, including local specialties, at good prices, and it's really nice to know who's growing your food. Ask lots of questions, especially if you see a new vegetable you don't know what to do with or want to know what's in season.

once you get it all home

Storing foods properly keeps them fresher for longer.

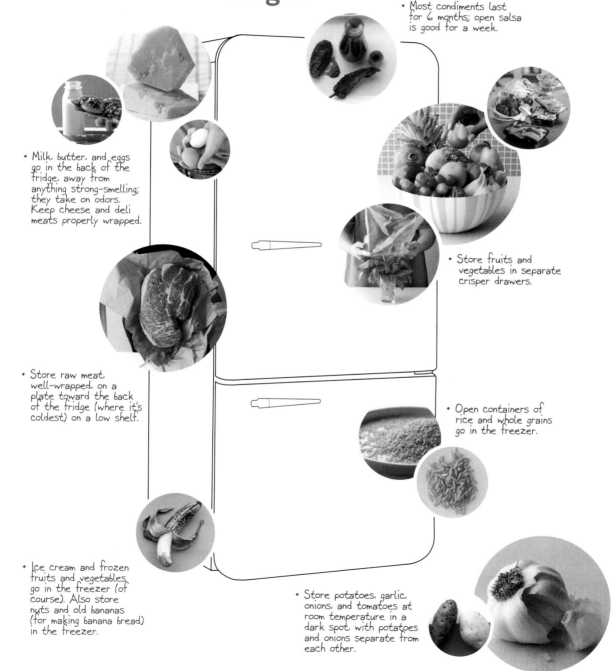

- Most condiments last for 6 months; open salsa is good for a week.

- Milk, butter, and eggs go in the back of the fridge, away from anything strong-smelling; they take on odors. Keep cheese and deli meats properly wrapped.

- Store fruits and vegetables in separate crisper drawers.

- Store raw meat, well-wrapped, on a plate toward the back of the fridge (where it's coldest) on a low shelf.

- Open containers of rice and whole grains go in the freezer.

- Ice cream and frozen fruits and vegetables go in the freezer (of course). Also store nuts and old bananas (for making banana bread) in the freezer.

- Store potatoes, garlic, onions, and tomatoes at room temperature in a dark spot with potatoes and onions separate from each other.

how to set up a pantry

Every pantry reflects the owner's individual taste—here's a list of basic spices and dry goods to get you started and upgrades to help you build your personal repertoire.

spices (basic)

kosher salt
whole black peppercorns
   (and a grinder)
red pepper flakes
dried herbs, like oregano,
   bay leaf, and thyme
ground cinnamon
whole nutmeg
a spice blend such as
   chili powder
   curry powder
   Italian seasoning
      or herbes de Provence
   five-spice powder

spices (upgrades)

ground cumin
ground coriander
paprika
fennel seeds
ground cardamom
ground allspice

condiments (basic)

[all of these go in the fridge
once open]
ketchup
mustard
hot sauce
jelly
salsa
soy sauce
Worcestershire sauce
real maple syrup

condiments (upgrades)

Asian chile pastes
sesame oil
hoisin sauce
chutney
fish sauce

dry goods (basic)

vegetable oil
extra-virgin olive oil
vinegar (see page 89)
chicken broth (canned
   or in paper containers)
nut butter
honey
pasta
canned tomatoes
rice
whole grains like
   oatmeal or bulgur
canned beans

dry goods (upgrades)

polenta
couscous
canned chiles
   (pickled jalapeños,
   chipotles en adobo)
jarred anchovies
tomato paste
bread crumbs
roasted peppers
sun-dried tomatoes

baking

all-purpose flour
baking powder
baking soda
sugar (white and brown)
pure vanilla extract
chocolate chips
cooking spray

salt & pepper

• Kosher salt is larger and flakier than table salt and about half as salty. We like kosher salt for savory food and table salt for sweet.
• Unsalted butter is best for cooking; it puts you in control of how much salt's in your food.
• Use a pepper grinder. Always. It doesn't need to be expensive—look for whole peppercorns packaged in a grinder in the spice aisle.

game plans: safety

It never hurts to know (check out foodnetwork.com for more detailed info):

cross-contamination

Most food poisoning comes from bacteria getting transferred from one thing (like raw chicken) to another (like salad). Here's how to avoid it:

- Wash your hands regularly before and during cooking with soap and warm water. Dry your hands with a clean, not dirty, towel.

- Wash everything (knives, cutting boards, spoons) that's touched raw ingredients too, especially poultry and meat.

- Run sponges through the dishwasher every so often to sanitize them.

- Proper storage goes a long way. Raw meats, chicken, and fish go in plastic bags, on plates, and away from cooked food, and must be refrigerated at all times. Your fridge should be below 40°F; use an appliance thermometer to check if you're not sure.

- Leftovers should be cooled and put in the fridge within 30 minutes of the end of a meal.

- Pork, chicken, and turkey should be fully cooked; use an instant-read thermometer to make sure. It should read between 145°F and 160°F for pork and between 165°F and 180°F for chicken and turkey. Beef and lamb are rare at 120°F and well done at 160°F.

the sharp & hot factor

Most things in your kitchen are one or the other—here's how to minimize the risk:

- Keep your knives sharp—the sharper they are, the better they get the job done. Besides, dull ones are more likely to slip and cut you. Don't leave sharp items in the sink and don't run with them in your hands (come on). If you cut yourself, clean and disinfect the cut, then cover it with a bandage.

- Grab hot pans with oven mitts or folded kitchen towels. Make sure your oven mitts are dry; water conducts heat superfast.

- In case of fire, deny oxygen. Smother the fire by covering the pan with a lid or pour on lots of salt or baking soda. **Never, ever, pour water on a kitchen fire.**

- Wear comfortable, well-fitting clothing and tie your hair back while cooking.

- If you burn yourself, don't put butter or oil on it. Cool it down with cold water or an ice pack, then apply antiseptic ointment and a bandage.

game plans: cooking

All that having been said—welcome to the kitchen! Here at FNK, we love food and we consider ourselves lucky to be able to share our passion for cooking with you. Our goal is to get you comfortable in the kitchen so that you can make everything from a quick after-work dinner to a once-a-year holiday feast with confidence and pride.

Everyone's got to start cooking somewhere. Let's get it started here.

Whether you have a tiny kitchen or a trophy kitchen, a little bit of planning goes a long way. If you're organized, you can turn out maximum taste from minimal space.

Read the recipe through before you start cooking, looking at both timing and ingredients:

timing

- An oven takes about 20 minutes to preheat; a large pot of water can take up to 15 minutes to boil. Save time by turning on the oven or putting the water on before you change out of your work clothes and start prepping for dinner.

ingredients

- Assemble everything you need before you start cooking; lay it all out in bowls on a pan or tray for mobility and easy access.

- Set up your cutting board equidistant from your stove and your sink for rapid rinsing and chop-and-drop. Put a damp paper towel underneath the cutting board to keep it in place.

- Keep salt, pepper, and whichever spices and cooking oil you're using within arm's reach.

- Keep a bowl for peelings and trimmings at your workspace to minimize trips to the garbage can.

- Do similar activities at once. For example, if you're making a salad, first peel all your veggies, then chop all of them—it's much quicker.

- Clean as you go! It makes all the difference in terms of both space and time.

breakfast

Quick, easy, and comforting, it starts the day better—and makes a great dinner too.

how to make coffee

Get a drip-style coffeemaker. It's easy: You barely have to do anything but remember this formula . . .

Markings on coffeepots can vary, so measure the amount of joe that your favorite mug takes, then fill the coffeemaker as needed. If this is too much to deal with in the morning, use fingernail polish to make your own markings on the pot.

to make	cold water	weak brew	strong brew
2 cups	2 cups	3 tablespoons ground coffee	1/3 cup ground coffee
4 cups	4 cups	1/3 cup ground coffee	3/4 cup ground coffee
8 cups	8 cups	3/4 cup ground coffee	1 cup ground coffee

a nice cup of tea

• Nothing beats the convenience of tea bags, but nothing beats the flavor of loose-leaf tea.
• If you're making black tea, the water should be just about to boil. For green, it should just start to steam. Pour the water over the bag or leaves (in a mesh ball for easy cleanup) to get the most out of 'em. Three minutes for black tea, one or two for green. If it goes too long, it'll taste harsh. Not a big deal, but not totally pleasant either.

TIPS

shopsmart

• If you like your coffee dark and heavy (coffee-chain style), go with a dark roast. For full-but-mellow flavor, go light.
• Freshness matters. Buy just as much as you need for a week. If you've got a choice between whole beans or preground, buy whole beans. Store them room temp in something airtight and grind them in a coffee grinder when you need them. One tablespoon of whole beans makes a slightly heaping tablespoon of ground. The finer the grind, the stronger the coffee.

caffeine wisdom

A regular cup of dark- or light-roast coffee has a little more caffeine than an espresso shot. Black tea has less and green tea, less than that.

it doesn't get much better than coffee and a carb.

toast

We all burn toast sometimes. It's the great kitchen equalizer. Don't worry about it.

It's the easiest breakfast on earth, and the best way to make something really good (breakfast) from a bad situation (rapidly staling bread).

And with all the kinds of bread out there, it's easy to have a high-style breakfast with no effort at all. Our favorite toppings? Butter, jam, honey, cinnamon sugar, cheese, olive tapenade, whatever's in the fridge and looks tasty . . .

No toaster? Use your oven's broiler or a grill pan, flipping with tongs when it looks done on a side.

tortillas

All tortillas—whether corn or flour—taste better when they're warmed up. Here's how:

On the stove: Turn the gas to low. Put the tortilla right on the burner and toast until it's lightly charred and puffy, flipping once with tongs, 10 to 15 seconds per side. If you've got an electric stove, do it in a dry skillet over medium-high heat.

In the microwave: Wrap the tortillas in slightly dampened paper towels and microwave on high until warm, about 15 seconds for one tortilla and about 45 seconds for a pack. If the tortillas are stuck together, microwaving the stack for 10 to 15 seconds makes them easier to pull apart.

bagels

Please don't hold a bagel in your hand while you cut it.

Here's a better way: Put the bagel flatter side down on a cutting board and keep it steady. Don't grip it—keep your fingers flat. Use a serrated knife to cut halfway through, then stand the bagel on the cutting board. Hold it from the top and finish cutting (see below).

start flat

then turn and slice downward

the ultimate grab-and-go begins and ends with fruit.

choose:

apples
Buy shiny-skinned red, yellow, or green apples without any soft spots.

bananas
Bananas should be light green to yellow (they'll ripen in a day or two), without any black spots.

berries
If you're buying strawberries, raspberries, blueberries, or black-berries in plastic boxes, check the bottom of the box for signs of squishing, juice, or mold—you don't want that.

citrus/tropicals
Grab an orange (or lemon or grapefruit or mango or papaya) in either hand and take the one that feels heavier.

grapes
Go with plump, full grapes without wrinkly skin or soft patches near the stem end.

melons
Melons like honeydew or cantaloupe should sound hollow when you tap them with your knuckles. Good cantaloupe usually has thick, raised "netting" (that is, texture) on the skin. Buy whole watermelon with a shriveled stem end and cut watermelon with a thin rind.

pears
Gently push pears in the neck with your finger; if they give a little, they're ripe.

pineapple
Pineapples should smell sweet, not boozy, and feel tender but not squishy. Or buy fresh pineapples that have been cored and peeled for you.

pomegranate
Look for large, shiny, and firm pomegranates with no cracks in their skin. Tap them; if you hear a metallic sound, they're ripe (see page 105 for how to deal with a pomegranate).

stone fruit
See stone fruits (peaches, plums, apricots, cherries) with the stems still attached? Buy them. Or check for a firm feel and a fruity smell.

fruit wisdom
· Keep most of your fruits out on the counter, except for apples, pears, berries, and stone fruit (like peaches, plums, or cherries), which should go in the crisper (away from the veggies).
· If you're trying to speed-ripen something (like pears, peaches, plums, or even avocados), put it in a paper bag with an apple for a day or two on the counter; apples give off gases that help fruit ripen faster. After it's ripe, store it in the refrigerator.
· The best time to wash any fruit (all you need is a quick rinse of water) is right before you eat it.
· There's a lot more variety in fruit than you'd think. Check out farmers' markets for wider selections of flavors, textures, and colors. Most supermarkets also carry precut fruit in plastic tubs, taking most of the work out of snacking.

TIPS

shopsmart
Buy fruit according to what's in season. Sure, you can get strawberries in the dead of winter and grapefruits in August, but when you do, you usually end up paying more for less flavor than when they're at their peak. Winter's for citrus; fall's for apples and pears; late spring's great for strawberries and pineapples; and summer's best for peaches, plums, blueberries, and melons.

the flexible smoothie serves 2 • prep time: 10 minutes

1   very ripe banana—frozen
    is great
1   cup frozen berries, such as
    strawberries, raspberries, or
    blackberries (about 6 ounces)
½   cup or one 6-ounce container
    plain, vanilla, or lemon low fat
    yogurt
½   cup orange juice, juice blend,
    or chilled green tea
2   ounces soft tofu (optional)
1   to 2 tablespoons honey,
    or to taste

Put everything in a blender and
puree until smooth. Pour into
2 tall glasses and serve.

**We're giving you a
smoothie recipe,
but you don't really
need one. Add whatever
you've got. You'll need:**

④ and if you
want, something
for health (like
wheat germ or
protein powder)

① something for body
(yogurt, tofu, soy
or regular milk)

② something for
flavor (fruit
orange juice,
honey, or
maple syrup)

③ something to
chill (frozen
fruit ice)

grown-up oatmeal serves 2 • prep time: 10 minutes

1   tablespoon unsalted butter
1   large pinch kosher salt
1½ to 1¾ cups water, or
      apple juice or cider
1   cup quick-cooking oats
1   orange or lemon
1   handful fresh or dried fruit
      like berries, sliced bananas,
      or apricots
      Brown sugar, honey, or maple
      syrup, for sprinkling
      Milk, plain yogurt, or kefir,
      for drizzling
1   handful nuts

1. Combine the butter, salt, and water or juice in a small saucepan and bring to a boil. Stir in the oats. Finely grate the citrus zest into the pan. Bring to a boil again, reduce to a simmer, and stir in fruit. Stir constantly until oats are cooked and dried fruit is slightly plumped, about 2 minutes.

▶ know-how 104

2. Divide into 2 bowls and sprinkle with sweetener of your choice (but taste first—if you use juice as your liquid, it may be sweet enough). Drizzle with milk or yogurt and top with nuts.

nut wisdom
Toasting nuts brings out all of their flavors and richness. To toast nuts, spread them out on a cookie sheet in a low oven (around 300°F) and cook until you can smell them, about 10 minutes.

TIPS

cook's note
Oatmeal makes it easy to start your day with healthy whole grains, and though quick-cooking oats require a little more effort than instant, they pay off in terms of texture and nutrition. In Food Network Kitchens, we make a lot of quick-cooking oats and top them with whatever it takes to get us going: fruit, honey, maple syrup, butter, nuts, kefir (a kind of liquid yogurt), or chocolate chips.

shopsmart
Try to stick to yogurts without a lot of sugar or flavorings. Plain's always a good way to go. You can always add honey, brown sugar, or maple syrup.

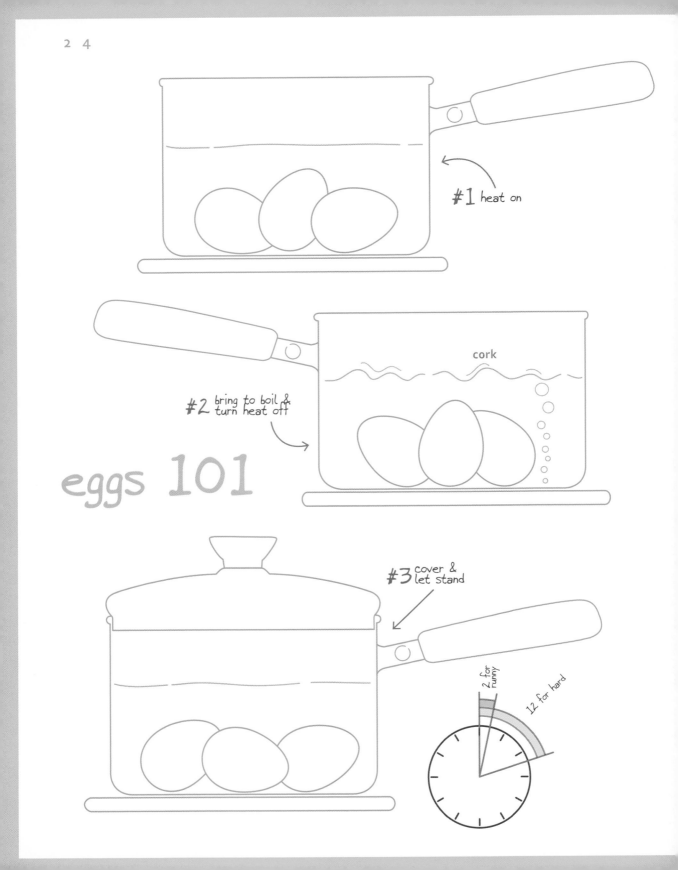

#1 heat on

cork

#2 bring to boil &
turn heat off

eggs 101

#3 cover &
let stand

2 for runny

12 for hard

breakfast and beyond
Eggs are one of the quickest, easiest ways to get a protein boost when you're feeling snackish or sluggish.

the best boiled egg

Put the eggs in a saucepan and cover them with about an inch of water. Bring the water to a boil, then cover the pan and shut off the heat. (Don't boil the eggs; that's what gets you a green ring and a sulphury taste in the yolk.) Let the whole thing sit for 2 to 12 minutes, depending how you like your eggs (2 minutes for runny yolks, 12 for hard), then run the eggs under cold water to stop the cooking and peel.

How to peel? If soft, crack off the end and scoop out the inside with a spoon. If they're hard, roll the egg on the counter to crack, then peel under running water.

Soft-boiled eggs make any breakfast feel luxurious, whether smeared on toast or savored with a spoon. Hard-boiled eggs keep (unpeeled) for a week in the fridge and are great for packed lunches or diced into any kind of salad, including the egg salad on page 52.

get good eggs
Open the carton and make sure the shells are undamaged and not stuck to the carton. Eggs come in different sizes; we use large in all our recipes.

keep 'em cool
Store your eggs in the coldest part of the fridge (that is, the back) and they'll last at least two weeks. They do pick up other scents and flavors easily, so keep them in the carton.

brown vs. white
There's no difference between brown and white eggs, health- or taste-wise. It's just a matter of the breed of chicken—though brown eggs do cost more. Regular eggs are great, but organic or farm-fresh are incredible.

cooking times
The longer you cook eggs, the eggier they get (not in a good way). So if the flavor and texture are too much for you, try cooking them less. They'll be creamier and milder and tastier.

for the health-conscious
And they're good for you. You can probably eat at least five eggs a week without worrying about it. If you do worry about it, ditch the yolks.

soft-boiled egg

overly easy fried eggs serves 1 • prep time: 7 minutes

1   teaspoon extra-virgin olive oil
2   large eggs
    Kosher salt and freshly ground
     black pepper

1. Brush a medium nonstick skillet (with a tight-fitting lid, preferably glass, so you can watch the eggs cook) with the oil and crack the eggs, side by side, into the skillet. Season with some salt and black pepper and set over medium heat. Cook until the outer edge of the whites turn opaque, about 1 minute.

2. Cover and adjust the heat to low. (Covering the eggs here keeps the steam in the pan, cooking the tops of the eggs so you don't have to flip them.) Cook until the eggs are done to your liking: 4 minutes for over-easy; 5 minutes for medium; or 6 minutes for hard. (Don't lift the lid.) Uncover and slide the eggs onto a serving dish.

upgrades

Sprinkle the eggs with a small pinch of cayenne, cumin, coriander, or chili powder for added flavor. If you like, serve with sliced tomatoes, Fresh Tomato Salsa (page 40), or Roasted Potatoes with Garlic & Parsley (page 212).

cook's note

TIPS

• For 2 people, use 4 eggs, a 10-inch skillet, and 2 teaspoons olive oil. Cook, uncovered, for 2 minutes until whites are opaque, then cover and follow other cook times.

• For 4, use 8 eggs, a 12-inch skillet, and a tablespoon of olive oil. Space yolks evenly in the skillet, with one in the center and seven around the outside. Cook, uncovered, for 4 minutes, then cover and cook for 6 minutes for over-easy, adding 1 minute for medium, and another minute for hard. To serve, slide the whole thing onto a large platter, and cut around the egg in the middle and then between each egg on the outside.

poached eggs

serves 1 to 4 • prep time: 10 minutes

1½ to 3 tablespoons light-colored
  vinegar, such as white, rice,
  cider, or white wine
2   to 8 large eggs
  Kosher salt and freshly ground
  black pepper

1. Fill a nonstick skillet with about
2 inches of water. (Use an 8-inch
skillet for 2 to 4 eggs, an 11-inch
for more than 4). Bring the water
to the barest simmer over medium-
low heat. Add 1½ tablespoons
vinegar for a smaller skillet or
3 tablespoons for a larger one.

2. To make sure the yolk doesn't
break, gently crack an egg into a
cup. Turn the cup, gently slipping
the egg into the water. Repeat with
the remaining eggs, placing the
eggs in a clockwise pattern in the
simmering water. Cook until the
whites are set but the yolks are still
runny, about 4 minutes per egg.

3. Fold up a double thickness of
paper towels and set on the counter.
Lift the eggs out of the water with
a slotted spoon and blot on the
towels. Gently transfer to a plate
and season each egg with salt and
black pepper to taste.

poached egg wisdom

To poach means to cook gently in
simmering water. Egg poaching is
tricky and takes a couple of tries
until you get the hang of it. Once
you do, though, poached eggs are
great for brunches. Cook them in
advance, keep them in cold-water-
filled plastic containers or a large
bowl in the fridge, and heat them
up in simmering water when ready
to serve. Fresh eggs poach best.

TIPS

don't panic
• Egg fell apart? There might not be enough vinegar in
the water, or the water may have been boiling too hard.
•Yolk broke? It might've been treated too roughly. Go
gentle on these; a nonstick spatula works wonders.
• Stuck to the pan? The pan might not be nonstick.
Lightly brush regular pans with oil before adding water.

scrambled eggs serves 2 to 4 • prep time: 8 minutes

2 to 3 large eggs per person
A little less than a tablespoon milk per egg
Kosher salt and freshly ground black pepper
1 tablespoon unsalted butter

1. Crack the eggs into a medium bowl. Add the milk and season with some salt and black pepper. Mix with a fork until there are no streaks of thick white.

2. Set a platter or a couple of plates by the stove or in a warm oven. Depending on how many eggs you're cooking, heat a medium or large nonstick skillet over medium-high heat. When the pan is just hot, add the butter (it should sizzle gently). Swirl the pan to distribute the butter as it melts. When the butter stops sizzling and the foam subsides, add the eggs. Pause to let the eggs heat slightly, then stir very slowly so the eggs cook evenly into large, fluffy curds. Cook, continuing to stir, for 2 to 6 minutes, depending on how set you like your eggs, but don't let the eggs brown. Transfer to the warm platter or plates and serve.

upgrades

Add chopped fresh herbs to raw eggs or add diced ham or cheese as the eggs set.

migas serves 4 • prep time: 15 minutes

1 small link Spanish chorizo sausage (about 2 ounces)
1 ripe plum tomato
1 small onion
1 clove garlic
Handful fresh cilantro sprigs
8 large eggs
1 teaspoon kosher salt, plus more for seasoning
3 tablespoons olive oil
4 6-inch stale corn tortillas
½ cup shredded Monterey Jack cheese (about 2 ounces)
Freshly ground black pepper

for serving:
chipotle hot sauce

1. Chop the chorizo. Halve the tomato crosswise, squeeze out seeds and discard, then chop the tomato. Peel and chop onion and garlic. Wash, dry, and chop cilantro.

▶ know-how 105, 99, 103

2. Crack eggs into a medium bowl, add the 1 teaspoon salt, and lightly beat.

3. Heat oil in a large nonstick skillet over medium heat. Break the tortillas into bite-size pieces and add to the skillet. Cook, turning until golden and a little crisp, about 3 minutes.

4. Add the chorizo, tomato, onion, and garlic and cook until the onion is soft, about 4 minutes. Pour the egg over all the vegetables and tortillas. Cook as for scrambled eggs. When eggs are still just soft, remove the pan from the heat and fold in the cheese and cilantro and season with salt and black pepper to taste. Serve with hot sauce.

a side of history

TIPS Migas, from the Spanish for "crumbs," are a classic Texan breakfast, originally eaten during Lent. Because of their connection to Lent, they're often vegetarian, so don't worry if you can't find chorizo.

breakfast meats

skillet bacon
prep time: 6 to 10 minutes

8   ounces bacon

1. Separate the strips of bacon and lay them in a single layer in heavy-bottomed skillet. (Bacon and a cast-iron skillet are a match made in heaven.) Set the pan over medium heat and cook until the bacon shrivels some and browns on the bottom, about 3 minutes. Turn the strips over and rotate them from the outside of the pan to the inside. Cook on the other side about 3 minutes for just-crisp bacon to 6 minutes for crispy throughout.

2. Drain cooked bacon on a plate lined with paper towels. Blot with more paper towels if needed and serve hot or at room temperature. (Reserve the pan drippings for cooking eggs, potatoes, or onions.)

baked bacon
prep time: 20 minutes

8   ounces bacon

1. Preheat the oven to 375°F.

2. Separate the strips of bacon and lay them in a single layer on a rimmed baking sheet. Bake the bacon to the desired degree of crispiness, about 15 minutes for just crisp and 18 minutes for crispy throughout. Drain cooked bacon on a plate lined with paper towels. Blot with more paper towels if needed and serve hot or at room temperature. (Reserve the pan drippings for cooking eggs, potatoes, or onions.)

canadian bacon
prep time: 5 minutes

4   slices Canadian bacon
1   teaspoon olive oil or butter

Heat a large skillet over medium heat and add the olive oil or butter. Lay the Canadian bacon in the hot skillet and cook, turning once, until browned on both sides, 4 to 5 minutes. Serve hot or at room temperature.

breakfast sausage
prep time: 8 minutes

8   ounces breakfast sausage
     (8 links)
2   tablespoons water
½   tablespoon unsalted butter

Place the sausage in a skillet just large enough to hold them in a single layer. Add the water, cover, and cook over medium heat for 3 minutes. Uncover, add the butter, and increase the heat to high. Cook until sausage is golden and butter just begins to brown, about 4 minutes. Serve hot.

TIPS

shopsmart
Breakfast link sausage comes either precooked or raw and is usually made with either chicken or pork. The precooked kind only needs heating; the raw kind needs to be cooked through.

shopsmart
Look for bacon with more red than white or buy center-cut for the best meat-to-fat ratio. Canadian bacon is sliced cured pork loin and is leaner than the streaky regular kind.

pancakes makes 8 large or 12 small pancakes • prep time: 15 minutes

1½ cups all-purpose flour
3 tablespoons sugar
1 tablespoon baking powder
½ teaspoon fine salt

Pinch freshly grated nutmeg (optional)
2 large eggs, at room temperature
1¼ cups milk

Dash pure vanilla extract (about ¼ teaspoon)
4 tablespoons (½ stick) unsalted butter
Canola oil or other neutral tasting oil, for cooking the pancakes

1. Preheat the oven to 200°F. Whisk together the flour, sugar, baking powder, salt, and nutmeg, if using, in a large bowl.

▶ know-how 107

2. Beat the eggs in another bowl. Whisk in about half the milk and the vanilla.

3. In a small saucepan over low heat, melt the butter with the remaining milk, stirring occasionally. Remove from heat. Stir or whisk into the egg mixture.

4. Pour the wet ingredients into the dry ingredients and whisk just until a thick batter forms (a few lumps are OK).

5. Heat a cast-iron skillet, nonstick skillet, or griddle over medium to medium-low heat (or 350°F, if the griddle temperature can be controlled). If using a cast-iron skillet or an older griddle, brush with canola oil. Keeping the skillet at medium to medium-low heat, ladle about ¼ cup (for small pancakes) to ⅓ cup (for large pancakes) of the batter onto the skillet. Make 1 or 2 more pancakes, spacing them evenly apart. Cook until bubbles break the surface of the pancakes, the batter loses its shine, and the undersides are golden brown, about 2 minutes. Slip the spatula under the pancakes and flip. Cook about 1 minute more. Serve immediately or transfer to a platter and keep warm in the oven. Repeat with the remaining batter.

pancake wisdom

· This batter is best slightly lumpy; perfectly smooth batter gets you hockey-puck pancakes.
· The first pancake's never quite right. The pan needs to even out its temperature first.
· Don't smash or push down on the pancakes while they're cooking; they'll get dense.
· Straight-to-plate is the best way to serve pancakes. If you've gotta wait, lay the pancakes out in a warm oven. Stacking them steams and toughens the middle ones.
· Top pancakes with berries, preserves, real maple syrup, honey, butter, yogurt, or a little whipped cream.

upgrades

When a pancake is brown on the first side and the top is bubbly, sprinkle on 2 teaspoons mini chocolate chips or toasted nuts, or 1 tablespoon diced bananas, whole blueberries, or grated apple. Flip gently and continue cooking until the pancake is cooked through, about 2 minutes more.

blueberry-lemon muffins makes 12 muffins • prep time: 45 minutes

2½ cups all-purpose flour
¾ cup white or light brown sugar,
   plus more for sprinkling
1 tablespoon baking powder
½ teaspoon fine salt
   Pinch of freshly grated nutmeg
½ cup vegetable oil
1 cup whole milk, at room
   temperature
2 large eggs, at room
   temperature
1 teaspoon pure vanilla extract
2 lemons
1½ cups fresh blueberries
   (about 1 pint)
Equipment: 12-cup standard muffin tin

1. Position a rack in the middle of the oven and preheat the oven to 375°F. Line twelve ½-cup muffin cups with paper liners.

2. Whisk the flour, sugar, baking powder, salt, and nutmeg together in a medium bowl. Whisk the oil, milk, eggs, and vanilla together in another bowl. Finely grate the zest from the lemons into the wet ingredients.

▶ know-how 107, 104

3. Make a small "well" or space in the center of the dry ingredients. Pour the wet ingredients and blueberries into the center. Stir wet and dry ingredients together with a spatula until dry ingredients are moistened but still a bit lumpy. (Do not overmix the batter or your muffins will be dense and tough.) Divide batter evenly among the muffin liners and sprinkle the tops generously with sugar (about ½ teaspoon per muffin).

4. Bake until golden brown and a toothpick inserted in the centers comes out clean, 25 to 30 minutes, rotating the pan halfway through cooking. Cool muffins in the pan on a rack for 5 to 10 minutes. Turn the muffins out of the pan and cool on the rack. Serve warm or at room temperature.

muffin wisdom

• We can't stress it enough: Mix the batter as little as possible. Overmixing leads to tough muffins and collapsed tops.
• If you used a light hand but the tops still collapse, it's probably your baking powder. Mix a pinch of your powder with hot water to test it. If it fizzes, it's good; if not, toss it.
• Don't overfill the muffin pans— ½ to ⅔ full is fine. Use an ice cream scoop for even filling.
• If you don't have liners, lightly coat the muffin tins with butter, then dust them with flour, tapping the tin upside down on the counter to shake off any excess.

▶ know-how 109

• Keep leftover muffins in the freezer, then warm them up in the oven when you want them.

don't overstir

cook's note

TIPS Wrap the zested lemons in plastic wrap, refrigerate them and save for their juice.

chocolate chip-banana bread
makes 1 loaf (about 9 slices) • prep time: 1½ hours (plus 20 minutes to cool)

½   cup (1 stick) unsalted butter,
    plus more for the pan
1½ cups all-purpose flour, plus
    more for the pan
½   cup sugar
¾   teaspoon baking soda
½   teaspoon fine salt
¼   teaspoon ground cinnamon
3   very ripe bananas
1   large egg, at room temperature
⅓   cup plain yogurt, whole
    or low fat
1   teaspoon pure vanilla extract
1   cup chocolate chips
¾   cup walnut pieces

Equipment: 9x5x3 metal loaf pan

very ripe banana

1. Position a rack in the center of the oven and preheat to 350°F. Butter and flour a loaf pan.
▶ know-how 109

2. Melt the ½ cup butter in a small saucepan over medium heat or covered in a microwave-safe bowl or measuring cup in the microwave. Cool slightly.

3. Whisk the flour, sugar, baking soda, salt, and cinnamon together in a large bowl.
▶ know-how 107

4. Mash the bananas with a fork in a medium bowl. Beat the egg in a small bowl with a fork or a whisk, then mix into the bananas. Mix in the yogurt, vanilla, and butter. Stir the wet ingredients into the dry ingredients until just combined. Stir in chocolate chips and

walnuts just as the batter comes together. Do not overmix the batter or your bread will be dense and tough; the batter should be wet, sticky, and a little lumpy. Scoop the batter into the prepared pan.

5. Bake until a toothpick inserted in the center of the loaf comes out clean, 65 to 70 minutes. The bread should rise in the middle to a crown, feel springy when touched, and pull away from the sides of the pan.
▶ know-how 108

6. Cool in the pan on a rack for at least 20 minutes before running a knife along the sides, unmolding, and slicing.

TIPS

cook's note
• If your bananas are fading to black (the darker, the sweeter), toss them in a plastic bag and keep them in the freezer until you have enough for this bread or the smoothie on page 22.

• All muffin wisdom applies to breads like this one, especially the overmixing part. Baking soda has the same shelf life as baking powder (about 6 months). Mix a pinch up with a little vinegar to check. If it foams, it's good. Old baking soda can go down the drain. Add a splash of vinegar (it will foam) to clean out the system.

snacks

Whether it's after school or at a party, everybody snacks. You can munch on these with pride.

popcorn three ways: cheese/sweet & spicy/rocky road **38** spiced nuts **39** spiced edamame **39** fresh tomato salsa **40** quesadillas **41** real guacamole **42** nachos **43** dips: blue cheese/italian bean/curry **45** bruschetta **46**

snack wisdom

There are two major categories of snack: the quick-and-easy tide over, generally eaten by oneself between meals, and the somewhat fancier bowl-of-something-nice for guests and parties. If it's a between-meals thing, keep it small and reasonably healthful or balance out a high cal ingredient (like nuts) with a lower cal one (like an apple). For guests, well, the sky's the limit.

some of our favorite quick between-meal snacks:

- Nuts and seeds: spiced, smoked, in trail-mix form, or plain
- Olives, ideally not canned
- Fruit, fresh or dried (check out dried apples, cranberries, or cherries)
- Peanut or other nut butters (like almond or soy) spread on everything
- Chocolate (with pretzels, or frozen bananas, or peanut butter, or by itself)
- Chocolate spreads for bread and fruit
- Cream cheese and hot pepper jelly (or spiced olives) on crackers
- Salsa (homemade on page 40 if you have time; jarred if you don't)
- Various types of sausage: Hungarian or Italian salami or Spanish-style chorizo
- Jarred pickled veggies (cucumbers, green beans, cauliflower, okra)
- Good-quality cheese: Sharp cheddar, fresh goat cheese, creamy blue cheese, Parmesan, and Brie are basics. If you've got a good cheese counter, explore it.
- World snacks from ethnic markets: Thai shrimp chips, Indian snack mix, or Hispanic- or Caribbean-style plantain chips

It's always a nice touch to serve snacks when people drop by; it works wonders to make them feel at home. Guacamole (page 42) or the dips on page 45 are great for guests because they're quick, easy, and give you lots of room to experiment with flavors of both dip and dippers: Raw vegetables, fruit, pita chips, and regular potato chips are all excellent.

Snacking's a great way to try new foods and combinations to find out what works for you. And if what you like ends up being something wacky, like hummus and ice cream, don't worry: No one's watching.

popcorn three ways each recipe serves 2 to 4 • prep time: 5 minutes

cheese popcorn

1   3.5-ounce package natural microwave popcorn (not the buttered kind)
1   clove garlic
1   tablespoon extra-virgin olive oil
½   teaspoon crushed red pepper flakes
1   teaspoon dried oregano or Italian seasoning
2   tablespoons freshly grated Parmesan cheese
    Kosher salt

1. Pop the popcorn according to package instructions. While hot, carefully open package and pour into a large bowl.

2. Smash the garlic clove and put it, the olive oil, pepper flakes, and dried herbs in a small microwave-safe bowl (a coffee mug is fine). Microwave on HIGH until the garlic browns, about 1 minute. Remove the garlic and drizzle the flavored oil over the popcorn. Toss the popcorn with your hands to coat. Add the cheese and toss again. Season to taste with salt. Serve hot.

▶ know-how 99

sweet & spicy popcorn

1   3.5-ounce package natural microwave popcorn (not the buttered kind)
2   tablespoons dark brown sugar
1   tablespoon butter
1   teaspoon chili powder

1. Pop the popcorn according to package instructions. While hot, carefully open package and pour into a large bowl.

2. Put the brown sugar, butter, and chili powder in a microwave-safe bowl; microwave on MEDIUM (50% power) until butter melts, about 1 minute. Stir to dissolve sugar. Drizzle over freshly popped popcorn; toss to evenly coat. Serve hot.

rocky road popcorn

1   3.5-ounce package natural microwave popcorn (not the buttered kind)
1½   cups mini chocolate chips
2   cups mini marshmallows
1   cup salted peanuts (optional)

1. Pop the popcorn according to package instructions. While it's still hot, carefully open package and pour popcorn into a large microwave-safe bowl. Stir in the chips and marshmallows.

2. Put bowl in microwave. Cook on HIGH until the chips and marshmallows get gooey, about 1 minute. Toss with a spoon, adding the peanuts, if using, until all the popcorn is coated. Set aside until the chocolate hardens, about 20 minutes. Serve.

microwave wisdom

Everyone's microwave is a little bit different. We've tried to give general directions here, but if yours needs a little more or less time to get the job done, adjust the recipe accordingly.

shopsmart

TIPS We're asking for nonbuttered popcorn here; it keeps the flavor neutral and lets you determine how many calories you want.

spiced nuts makes 2 cups • prep time: 50 minutes

Vegetable oil
1 egg white
1 tablespoon Cajun seasoning or Madras curry powder
3 tablespoons sugar
2 cups salted, roasted mixed nuts

1. Preheat the oven to 250°F. Lightly oil a rimmed baking sheet.

2. Whisk the egg white, Cajun seasoning or curry powder, and sugar in a medium bowl until thoroughly blended and slightly foamy. Add the nuts and toss to coat evenly. Spread nuts on the prepared baking sheet and roast, stirring every 15 minutes, for

▶ know-how 108

45 minutes. Nuts will be fragrant and slightly darker but still a bit moist. They'll crisp as they cool. Cool completely in the pan and serve at room temperature. Nuts will keep in an airtight container for up to 5 days.

spiced edamame serves 4 to 6 as an appetizer, 10 as party food • prep time: 10 minutes

1 1-pound bag frozen edamame, in the pod (green soybeans)
2 teaspoons kosher salt, plus more for seasoning
1 teaspoon chili powder
¼ teaspoon crushed red pepper flakes
½ teaspoon dried oregano

edamame

1. Bring a medium pot of water to a boil. Season with some salt. Add the edamame pods and cook, uncovered, until heated through and crisp-tender, 5 to 6 minutes. Drain in a colander and pat dry.

2. While the edamame boil, heat the 2 teaspoons kosher salt, chili powder, and pepper flakes in a small dry skillet over medium heat,

stirring until hot and fragrant, about 2 minutes. Remove from the heat and crumble in the oregano. Toss the drained edamame pods with the chili salt. Serve warm with a side bowl on the table for the empty pods.

cook's note

TIPS Edamame are green soybean pods. They're low fat, high-protein, and tasty. You'll see them steamed and salted wherever sushi is sold or precooked in the frozen food section of your supermarket. To eat them, pick them up with your fingers, put the pod in your mouth, and squeeze the inner seeds out with your teeth. Discard the outer pod once you've gotten all the seeds out.

fresh tomato salsa serves 4 to 6 • prep time: 5 minutes

2   ripe tomatoes (about 1 pound)
    or 1 pint grape or cherry
    tomatoes (whichever smell or
    taste better when shopping)
1½ teaspoons kosher salt
¼   small white or red onion
1   small clove garlic
1   to 2 jalapeños
    Handful of fresh cilantro leaves
    with some stems, fresh mint
    leaves, or both (about ¼ cup)

for serving:
tortilla chips or quesadillas
    (see opposite page)

1. If using large tomatoes, halve them and grate the cut side on the largest holes of a box grater into a bowl all the way down to the skins. Discard skins. If using grape or cherry tomatoes, just quarter them. Season with half the salt. Grate the onion into the tomato.

2. Smash the garlic clove, sprinkle with a pinch of salt, and, with the flat side of a large knife, mash and smear the mixture to a coarse paste. Halve the jalapeños lengthwise and remove stems. Chop the jalapeños very finely. (For a mild salsa, scrape out the seeds with the tip of your knife before chopping. For more heat, leave the seeds in.) Chop the cilantro and stir into the salsa. Season with the rest of the salt. Serve with chips or Quesadillas (opposite).

▶ know-how 99, 103

chile wisdom

Taking the ribs (the white parts on the inside) and seeds out of chiles lessens the burn. The smaller the variety of chile, the hotter, so keep that in mind. See page 99 for more information on working with chiles.

upgrades

Add some chopped ginger, or a squeeze of lime juice, or drizzle of olive oil.

 TIPS

cook's note
Leftover salsa's a great topping for chicken, fish, pork, or eggs, so it pays off to make extra.

quesadillas serves 4 to 6 • prep time: 8 minutes

- 4 to 6 tablespoons unsalted butter
- 8 small flour or corn tortillas
- 8 ounces sliced or shredded cheese, such as Cheddar, Monterey Jack, Gouda, or Brie

for serving:
fresh tomato salsa
 (see opposite page)

Melt about half a tablespoon of butter in a small skillet over medium to medium-low heat. Put a tortilla in the skillet and scatter just enough cheese on top to cover the tortilla (about 1 ounce). Cook until tortilla softens, about 1 minute, then fold the tortilla in half and cook on each side until golden brown, adding a peanut-size nub of butter as needed, about 4 minutes more. Repeat with remaining ingredients. Cut the quesadillas into wedges and serve with Fresh Tomato Salsa (opposite).

upgrades
Add a small handful of cooked shredded chicken or pork, roasted peppers or other veggies, chopped cilantro, or a sprinkling of chili powder or cumin to the cheese.

cook's note
TIPS If you're making a lot of quesadillas, use several skillets to speed up the process. If you only have one skillet, keep the quesadillas warm in a 200°F to 250°F oven as you make them.

shopsmart
Corn or flour tortillas? Corn are heartier and healthier; flour are softer and easier to wrap with. It's up to you.

real guacamole serves 2 to 3 (double or triple for a party) • prep time: 10 minutes

¼   small red onion
1   jalapeño or 5 slices pickled
    jalapeño
1   ripe Hass avocado
1   lime
½   teaspoon kosher salt
    Ground cumin (optional)
    Ground coriander (optional)

for serving:
tortilla chips

1. Chop the onion into very small pieces. Halve the jalapeño lengthwise and remove the stem. For a milder dip, scrape out the seeds with the tip of your knife; for more heat, leave the seeds in. Chop the chile very finely. (If using the pickled jalapeños, finely chop.)

▶ know-how 99

2. Halve and seed the avocado. Scoop the flesh from the shell with a spoon into a medium bowl. Squeeze lime juice over avocado and stir to coat evenly. Add onion and jalapeño along with salt and a pinch of cumin and coriander, if using. Use a fork to stir and mash into chunky guacamole. Serve with tortilla chips.

▶ know-how 106

upgrades

Add a handful chopped fresh cilantro, a diced tomato or mango, or a handful of quartered seedless grapes.

TIPS   **cook's note**
Avocados are almost never ready to eat when you buy them, so the best guacamole does require a little bit of advance planning. Buy the wrinkly Hass avocados, keep 'em in a paper bag at room temperature, and add an apple to the bag to speed up the ripening. When they're ready they should be soft (but not squishy) to the touch, and you should be able to flick the little stem off easily. And nothing keeps an avocado green for long once cut, so eat it ASAP.

nachos serves 6 to 8 • prep time: 20 minutes

5   scallions (white and green parts) or ½ small red onion
1   15-ounce can black or pinto beans
2   to 3 whole pickled jalapeños
     Cooking spray
8   ounces white corn tortilla chips (half of a large bag)
12   ounces shredded Cheddar cheese (about 3 cups)
1½   teaspoons kosher salt
1   large ripe tomato
     Handful of fresh cilantro leaves with some stems
     Sour cream, for garnish

1. Preheat the oven to 400°F. Thinly slice the scallions or chop the onion. Rinse and drain beans in a colander. Chop the jalapeños.

▶ know-how 99

2. Lightly spray a rimless baking sheet or a double or triple layer of foil with cooking spray. Scatter the chips evenly over the pan or foil. Scatter the scallions or onions, beans, jalapeños, and cheese over the chips. Season with ½ teaspoon of the salt.

3. Bake the nachos until the cheese melts and begins to brown on the edges, 12 to 15 minutes.

4. Meanwhile, chop the tomatoes and cilantro and toss in a bowl with the remaining salt.

▶ know-how 105, 103

5. Slip a metal spatula or knife under the hot nachos to free them from the pan or foil. Then slide the nachos onto a cutting board or large platter. Scatter the tomatoes on top and top the nachos with dollops of sour cream. Serve hot.

TIPS

cook's note
The best nachos are an excuse to eat whatever you want with chips as a vehicle. Think leftover diced chicken, extra veggies, shredded lettuce, fresh chiles, a couple different kinds of cheese, shrimp . . .

shopsmart
Canned pickled jalapeños tend to have a milder, mellower flavor than fresh ones, and a splash of the juice from the can adds vinegary pucker to soups, stews, and salad dressings.

It's simple, quick, and impressive to make your own dips, and you can experiment pretty freely with dippers. Instead of potato or tortilla chips, try cut-up raw vegetables, pita triangles, or bread sticks.

dips

each of these serves 4 to 6 • prep time for each dip: 10 minutes • *Equipment: food processor (for all)*

blue cheese dip

6	sprigs fresh flat-leaf parsley
½	lemon
¼	red onion or 1 shallot
	Worcestershire sauce
¾	cup sour cream or plain yogurt
½	cup mayonnaise
4	ounces crumbled blue cheese
1	teaspoon kosher salt
	Freshly ground black pepper

for serving:
chips or fresh vegetables

1. Strip the parsley leaves from the stems. Zest the lemon. Roughly chop the onion or shallot.

▶ know-how 103, 104, 99

2. Put the parsley, zest, and onion or shallot in a food processor. Squeeze in the juice of the lemon and a few dashes of the Worcestershire sauce and process to a paste. Add the sour cream, mayonnaise, blue cheese, salt, and black pepper to taste and pulse until combined. Serve immediately with chips or vegetables or refrigerate until ready to serve.

italian bean dip

3	cloves garlic
2	sprigs fresh rosemary, sage, or thyme, or a combination
⅓	cup extra-virgin olive oil
	Pinch crushed red pepper flakes
1	15-ounce can Great Northern beans or chickpeas
	Kosher salt

1. Smash garlic cloves. Strip the leaves off the herb stems and discard the stems.

▶ know-how 99, 103

2. Warm the garlic and the olive oil in a small pan or skillet over medium-high heat, stirring, until the garlic is golden, about 3 minutes. Remove from heat and add the herbs and red pepper flakes to the hot oil. Cool slightly.

3. Rinse and drain the beans. Put the beans and all but 1 tablespoon of the garlic-herb oil in a food processor. Season with a couple pinches of salt and puree until smooth. Scrape dip into a serving bowl and drizzle with reserved garlic-herb oil.

curry dip

2	cloves garlic
1	4-inch piece fresh ginger
1	tablespoon unsalted butter or vegetable oil
2	tablespoons Madras curry powder (see page 141)
1	scallion (white and green parts)
6	sprigs fresh cilantro
2	tablespoons sweet mango chutney
¾	cup sour cream or plain yogurt
½	cup mayonnaise
1	lime
1	teaspoon kosher salt
	Freshly ground black pepper or hot sauce

1. Smash and then chop the garlic. Peel the ginger and slice into coins.

▶ know-how 99

2. Heat the butter over medium heat in a small saucepan. Add the garlic and ginger and cook until fragrant, about 2 minutes. Add the curry powder; cook, stirring, until fragrant, about 30 seconds more. Let cool to room temperature.

3. Meanwhile, roughly chop the scallion and cilantro. Put the curry mixture in a food processor along with the scallion, cilantro, chutney, sour cream, and mayonnaise. Cut the lime in half and squeeze in the lime juice. Process to make a smooth paste. Season with the 1 teaspoon salt and black pepper or hot sauce to taste. Cover and refrigerate until serving.

▶ know-how 99, 103

bruschetta serves 4 to 6 • prep time: 5 minutes

1 loaf French bread or coarse country bread Extra-virgin olive oil	Kosher salt 1 large clove garlic

1. Preheat the broiler or a stovetop grill pan to high.

2. Use a serrated knife to slice the bread crosswise on a sharp angle to get broad slices about ½ inch thick. Drizzle both sides very lightly with olive oil and season with salt to taste. If using a broiler, lay the bread on a baking sheet.

3. Toast the bread under the broiler or on the grill pan until the edges char a bit and the surface is golden. Turn and toast the other side. Smash and peel the garlic. Rub the clove all over the surface of the toasted bread to flavor it. Serve warm or at room temperature.

▶ know-how 99

upgrades

In Italian, *bruschetta* means roasted over coals—but grilling or broiling is fine. Garlic and olive oil is the classic topping, but no one's going to look at you funny for experimenting. Try a dollop of good-quality fresh ricotta, storebought pesto or tapenade, sautéed mushrooms, our Italian Bean Dip (page 45) or the Little Tomato Salad (page 87), or a smear of soft cheese, like Brie, goat cheese, or soft herb cheese. We also like it topped with lightly dressed arugula and thin slices of good ham or prosciutto or a piece of smoked fish.

shopsmart
Good bread is key here. What do we mean by good bread? Something with character, crust, and color. Something that smells yeasty and inviting. If you've got a bakery nearby, check out its bread, or try those "freshly baked" breads at the grocery store.

sandwiches

Stacked, stuffed, or rolled, sandwiches are convenient, delicious, and totally portable.

sandwich wisdom

There's a world of sandwiches out there, from good old peanut butter and jelly or ham and cheese to banh mi (the Vietnamese hero, traditionally made with a few kinds of pork, pickled vegetables, cilantro, mayo, and hot chiles), the New Orleans classic muffuletta (olive salad, ham, salami, and provolone), and the everywhere-these-days panino (pressed-and-grilled ciabatta bread with assorted fillings).

Basically, everything tastes better in sandwich form, and we encourage you to run wild.

packing a lunch?
The key thing to remember is to keep hot foods hot and cold foods cold. To play it safe, ditch anything that's been held between 40°F and 140°F for longer than 2 hours and always keep cold foods and hot foods separate.

When you're packing a meal, take just as much food as you need so that you don't have to worry about keeping leftovers safe.

And there's nothing inherently wrong with packing mayo-based food to go, but you've got to be extra careful to keep the temperature where it should be.

cold food
Get yourself an insulated lunch bag and a refreezable gel ice pack. If you've got a fridge you can use for during-the-day storage, all the better.

hot food
Fill an insulated bottle with boiling water, let it stand for a minute or two, then dump out the water and fill with hot soup, chili, pasta, or stew.

chicken or turkey salad sandwiches serves 4 • prep time: 8 minutes

½ a rotisserie chicken, 2 cooked
boneless skinless chicken
breasts, or about 12 ounces
turkey breast meat
something crunchy:
(1 rib celery, 1 small apple,
½ fennel bulb, 3 to 5 radishes,
or ½ cup sweet or dill pickle
slices)
something oniony:
(¼ small red onion, 2 scallions
[white and green parts],
or 1 large shallot)
½ cup mayonnaise
Kosher salt and freshly
ground black pepper
8 slices bread

1. Shred the chicken meat by hand, discarding any skin or bones, and put in a large bowl. You'll have about 1½ cups meat.

2. Chop the "something crunchy" (you'll have about ½ cup) and add to the bowl. Chop whatever onion you choose; add to the mix. Add the mayonnaise, salt, and black pepper to taste and stir until evenly coated. Add more salt and black pepper, if needed.

▶ know-how 100, 99

3. Lay 4 slices of bread on the counter; divide the salad evenly among them. Top with the remaining bread.

egg salad serves 4 • prep time: 8 minutes

5 large eggs
something crunchy:
(1 rib celery, 1 small apple,
½ fennel bulb, 3 to 5 radishes,
or ½ cup sweet or dill pickle
slices)
something oniony:
(¼ small red onion, 2 scallions
[white and green parts],
or 1 large shallot)
½ cup mayonnaise
Kosher salt and freshly
ground black pepper
8 slices bread

1. To cook the eggs: Put eggs in a small saucepan with enough cold water to cover. Bring to a boil, cover, and remove from the heat. Set aside for 10 minutes. While the eggs cook, chop the "something crunchy" (you'll have about ½ cup) and add to the bowl. Chop whatever onion you choose; add to the mix. Add the mayonnaise and salt and black pepper to taste and stir until evenly coated. Add more salt and black pepper, if needed.

▶ know-how 100, 99

2. Drain the eggs and roll them between your palm and the counter to crack the shell, then peel under cool running water. Coarsely chop the eggs; add to the bowl. Toss until evenly coated. Adjust seasoning with more salt and black pepper, if needed.

3. Lay 4 slices of bread on the counter; divide the salad evenly among them. Top with the remaining bread.

cook's note
You can also make tuna salad with a can of tuna and a little less mayonnaise than the recipes call for, or check out the tuna sandwich on page 54.

upgrades
Add thickly sliced tomatoes and lettuce to the sandwiches or stir in 2 tablespoons freshly chopped herbs, such as parsley or basil, or 2 tablespoons whole-grain mustard.

make it curried
Stir in 2 teaspoons curry powder, ⅓ cup chopped fresh cilantro, and ¼ cup golden raisins.

chicken or tuna or eggs + mayo + something crunchy
+ something oniony = salad (+ bread = sandwich)

"hold the mayo" tuna sandwich serves 4 • prep time: 40 minutes

dressing

2	anchovy fillets (optional)
2	tablespoons red wine vinegar
1/3	cup extra-virgin olive oil
1	teaspoon dried Italian seasoning or herbes de Provence
1	teaspoon kosher salt
	Freshly ground black pepper

sandwich

1/2	small red onion
2	6-ounce cans tuna, packed in oil
4	sun-dried tomatoes, packed in oil
2	jarred roasted red peppers
1	bunch arugula
3	tablespoons capers
1	French baguette (about 18 inches long)
1	clove garlic
1/4	cup pitted Kalamata olives
	Kosher salt and freshly ground black pepper

1. Make the dressing: Rinse the anchovies, if using; put in a bowl and mash to a paste with a fork. Whisk in the vinegar, then the olive oil, herbs, salt, and black pepper to taste. Set aside.

2. For the sandwich: Peel and slice the red onion as thinly as you can and soak in a bowl of cold water (soaking mellows the bite a bit). Meanwhile, drain the tuna and put in a bowl. Lightly toss with a couple of tablespoons of the dressing. Drain the sun-dried tomatoes and roasted peppers and slice them. Wash the arugula. Pat dry with paper towels and pull off any tough stems. Rinse and drain the capers.

▶ know-how 99

3. Halve the baguette lengthwise and pull out some of the insides to make a pocket. Lightly smash the garlic clove and rub over the cut side of the bread. Drizzle both halves with the remaining dressing. Drain the red onion and pat dry with paper towels.

▶ know-how 99

4. Layer the bottom half of the baguette with the sun-dried tomatoes, roasted peppers, arugula, tuna, onion, capers, and olives. Season with salt and black pepper to taste. Cover with the top of the baguette, press down lightly, and wrap tightly with plastic wrap. Set aside for 30 minutes or up to 2 hours for the flavors to come together.

5. Use a serrated knife or a saw-toothed steak knife to slice into 4 servings. (It's easier to slice while still wrapped.)

▶ know-how 99

TIPS shopsmart

• Herb blends like herbes de Provence (made of a blend of marjoram, thyme, rosemary, and lavender, and sometimes also basil and fennel) save you a lot of time and space by packing a variety of flavors into one jar. Look for them in the spice aisle.

• Oil-packed tuna is full of flavor and best for mayo-less sandwiches like this one, where you really want the tuna to shine. Anchovies are great—go with the oil-packed kind in clear glass jars for maximum convenience without skimping on taste.

chicken-avocado wrap with chipotle ranch dressing
serves 4 • prep time: 15 minutes

½ red onion
½ cup ranch dressing, bottled or homemade (page 91)
2 tablespoons chipotle salsa
1 orange
½ a roast or rotisserie chicken
1 ripe Hass avocado
1 ripe medium tomato
 Kosher salt and freshly ground black pepper
4 8-inch flour tortillas
2 handfuls prewashed lettuce leaves
4 sprigs fresh cilantro

1. Thinly slice the onion. Soak in a bowl of cold water (soaking mellows the bite a bit).
▶ know-how 99

2. Stir dressing and salsa together in a bowl. Finely grate zest of ¼ of the orange and stir into dressing.
▶ know-how 104

3. Pull meat from the chicken in small chunks and discard the skin. Halve, seed, and slice the avocado. Slice the tomato and sprinkle with some salt and black pepper.
▶ know-how 106, 105

4. Using tongs, warm each tortilla by holding over an electric or gas burner until soft and pliable (it's OK if it chars slightly). Lay the tortillas on a cutting board and spread about 2 tablespoons of the dressing over each tortilla, leaving about a 1-inch border around the edge. Layer the chicken, avocado, lettuce, tomato, and cilantro evenly over each tortilla, still leaving a border. Drain the onions, pat dry with a paper towel, and sprinkle over the wraps. Season with salt and black pepper to taste. Take both sides of the tortilla and fold about an inch on either side over the filling. Keeping the sides folded, tightly roll up the tortilla from the bottom into a cylinder. Halve, using a serrated knife if you have one, and serve.

wrap wisdom
A burrito is basically a wrap with a hot filling. Warm the tortilla and fill with leftover rice, beans, or guacamole—really, whatever—to make a meal.

make it your own
Instead of chicken, add the bean dip on page 45 or leftover roasted or grilled vegetables like zucchini, peppers, or mushrooms.

rolling wraps and burritos

cook's note
TIPS Soaking onions in cold water softens their bite, making them easier to eat raw.

shopsmart
Chipotles are smoked jalapeño peppers. You'll usually see them canned in adobo sauce in the spice section of your store or in bottled salsa form near the chips and dips. See page 161 for more information.

caprese salad sandwich
serves 4 • prep time: 5 to 10 minutes

12 ounces fresh salted mozzarella
    cheese
    Kosher salt and freshly ground
    black pepper
2   large ripe tomatoes (about
    1 pound)
8   slices good sourdough bread
1   clove garlic
1   tablespoon extra-virgin olive oil
    Handful of fresh basil leaves

1. Heat a stovetop grill pan or a broiler to high heat.

2. Slice the cheese about ¼ inch thick and season with salt and black pepper to taste. Core the tomatoes, slice crosswise the same thickness as the cheese, and season with some salt and black pepper.

▶ know-how 105

3. Grill or broil the slices of bread, turning as needed, until evenly toasted, about 1 minute. Lightly smash and peel the garlic. Rub 1 side of each slice of bread with the garlic. Drizzle with the olive oil. Roughly tear the basil leaves. Layer the cheese, basil, and tomatoes on 4 slices of bread and top with the remaining bread.

▶ know-how 99

TIPS

shopsmart
Fresh salted mozzarella (the white-ball kind) is key here for moisture and flavor. If it's sold floating in water, take it out of the water, wrap it in plastic wrap, and store it in the fridge to keep it firm and flavorful.

Or check the grocery store salad bar for bocconcini (bite-size fresh mozzarella balls). Fresh mozzarella's got a short shelf life (about 3 days), but the rich, creamy flavor makes it worth planning a meal around.

classic grilled cheese serves 1 • prep time: 5 minutes

½ ripe tomato or 1 plum
     tomato (optional)
2   thick slices white, whole
     wheat, or sourdough bread
2   to 3 slices Monterey Jack,
     cheddar, or Swiss cheese
     (about 1 ounce)
2   slices baked ham or cooked
     bacon (optional)
     Sliced dill or sweet pickles
     (optional)
1   tablespoon unsalted butter

1. If using the tomato, thinly slice it and let drain on paper towels for about 5 minutes.

2. Place a slice of bread on your cutting board. Layer half the cheese slices on the bread. Lay tomato, ham, or pickles, if using, on top of the cheese. Cover with the remaining cheese. Top with the other slice of bread and press down lightly.

3. Heat a medium skillet (we love cast iron for this) over medium-low heat and melt about half the butter. Carefully place the sandwich in the pan and cook until the bread toasts and the cheese is slightly melted, 3 to 5 minutes. Turn with a spatula and add the remaining butter. Cook until the other side is toasted and the cheese is melted, about 3 minutes more. If at any time the bread starts to brown too quickly, lower the heat to prevent the bread from scorching before the cheese melts.

upgrades
• Crisp-cooked bacon/cheddar/ sliced apple on black bread
• Muenster/red onion on sourdough
• Mozzarella/tomato/basil on ciabatta
• Salami/provolone/mustard on rye
• Ham/Gruyère on French bread
• Cheddar/tomato/onion/fresh cilantro on sturdy white bread
• Monterey Jack/pickled jalapeños/leftover shredded chicken on whole sgrain

(Oh, and what's a tuna melt but an open-faced grilled cheese? Make a tuna salad as suggested on page 52, then heap it on a slice of bread, top with your favorite cheese, put it on a baking sheet or some foil, and run the whole thing under the broiler until the cheese melts.)

TIPS
cook's note
This is comfort food at its most comforting. We like to use whatever cheese we've got around (and there's almost always something around) for these, but melty cheese is a deeply personal matter, so pick your favorite. Check out the options at your store's cheese section. There's a world of cheese out there.

bacon-cheddar sandwiches for a crowd
serves 4 • prep time: 25 minutes

8	slices bacon
4	scallions
8	slices potato sandwich bread

6	tablespoons unsalted butter, at room temperature
8	ounces sliced Cheddar cheese

1. Preheat the oven to 375°F. Lay the bacon in a single layer on a rimmed baking sheet and cook until crisp, about 15 to 20 minutes. Drain on paper towels. Cool and rinse the pan.

2. Line the baking sheet with foil. Trim the root ends of the scallions, halve lengthwise, and chop into about 1-inch pieces.

▶ know-how 99

3. Lay out the bread on a work surface and butter 1 side of each piece. Put 4 slices of the bread, buttered side down, on the prepared baking sheet. Layer half the cheese slices on the bread. Layer the bacon and scallions on top of the cheese and cover with the remaining cheese. Top with the remaining slices of bread buttered side up and bake until each bottom piece of bread is golden brown, about 10 minutes. Flip the sandwiches and bake until the other side is golden brown and cheese has melted, about 8 to 10 minutes more.

cheddar wisdom
Cheddar is a cow's-milk cheese that can be orange, white, mild, sharp, aged, or young. The cheese flavor gets sharper with age. If you like mild cheese, buy younger cheddar, sometimes labeled medium-sharp. The orange color comes from a plant-based food coloring that doesn't affect taste.

TIPS cook's note
These are great for groups; baking them in the oven means you're not anchored to the stove flipping sandwiches. Pair them up with a big pot of the chili on page 161. If your crowd is at all the type to get involved in the kitchen (older kids, willing friends, whatever), speed up the process by lining everyone up and putting sandwiches together assembly line style.

burgers serves 4 • prep time: 10 to 20 minutes

1½ pounds ground beef sirloin
1 teaspoon kosher salt
 Freshly ground black pepper
1 tablespoon vegetable oil

4 soft hamburger buns, split
4 slices cheese, such as Cheddar, American, Saga blue cheese, or Swiss (optional)

for serving:
lettuce leaves, sliced tomato, mustard, ketchup, and mayonnaise

1. Preheat the oven to 450°F.

2. Using your hands, break the meat into small pieces. Spread the meat out in an even layer on a pan or large plate. Season it generously with the salt and some black pepper. Divide the meat into 4 portions. Form each portion into a ball by gently tossing it from one hand to the other. (Don't overwork or press too firmly on the meat or the burgers will be tough, not juicy.) Gently form each portion into a patty about 1 inch thick.

3. Preheat a skillet, large enough to hold all 4 burgers without crowding, over medium-low heat for about 2 minutes. Raise the heat to medium high and add oil. Add the patties and cook until well browned, about 2 minutes. Turn patties over and transfer skillet to the oven. Cook to desired doneness: 7 to 8 minutes for medium rare; 9 to 11 minutes for medium or 13 to 15 minutes for well done. (For cheeseburgers, lay a slice of cheese on top of burgers during the last couple minutes so that it melts.)

4. While the burgers cook, place the buns on a baking sheet cut side up. Toast them in the oven until the tops are crisp and golden, about 3 minutes.

5. Transfer the hamburgers to a plate and let rest for a couple of minutes before serving. (For notes on resting meat, check out page 158.) Assemble the hamburgers with the condiments and toppings of your choice.

turkey burger

For either variation at right, mix 2 tablespoons plain yogurt into 1½ pounds ground turkey along with the salt and black pepper. These burgers are wetter than beef burgers, so spread cooking oil on your hands when making the patties. Turkey burgers must be cooked all the way through; follow our instructions for regular burgers, cooking for 15 minutes for well done.

upgrades

Here are two easy ways to bump up the flavor of your burger—particularly a good idea for turkey.

southwestern-style burger

Mix in 1 heaping teaspoon chili powder and a couple shakes of hot sauce along with the salt and black pepper. To serve, top with Monterey Jack cheese, sliced avocados, salsa, and fresh cilantro leaves on a soft roll.

pub burger

Mix in 2 teaspoons Worcestershire sauce and 2 tablespoons grainy mustard along with the salt and black pepper. To serve, top with extra-sharp English cheddar and serve on a toasted sandwich-size English muffin.

TIPS
cook's note

Ground sirloin is lower in fat and steakier tasting than chuck, which is why we use it. For a more classic burgery taste, go with a blend of the two. Cook beef burgers until a thermometer inserted sideways into the center of the burger reads 145°F for medium rare, 160°F for medium, and 170°F for well done. Poultry, on the other hand, needs to be cooked through, until it's between 170°F and 175°F.

buffalo chicken sub sandwiches serves 4 • prep time: 20 minutes

3 boneless, skin-on chicken
  breast halves (about
  1½ pounds)
2 teaspoons chili powder
  Kosher salt and freshly ground
  black pepper

6 tablespoons unsalted butter
1 to 2 ribs celery
½ bunch watercress
1 baguette (aka French bread,
  15 to 18 inches long)

4 tablespoons hot sauce
2 ounces creamy blue cheese,
  like Saga blue
¼ cup mayonnaise or sour cream

1. Preheat the oven to 350°F. Pat the chicken dry with paper towels and season all over with chili powder and some salt and black pepper. Heat a large skillet over medium-high heat; add 2 tablespoons of the butter. Lay the chicken skin side down in the skillet and cook without moving until the skin is golden and crispy, about 4 minutes. Turn and cook until the chicken is opaque, about 4 minutes more. Reserve the skillet. Put the chicken in a baking dish or roasting pan and bake until firm to the touch, about 10 minutes. Set

chicken aside to rest for 5 minutes before slicing.

2. While the chicken bakes, thinly slice the celery. Trim and discard the tough stems from the watercress. Rinse, dry, and set aside the leaves.

▶ know-how 100

3. Cut the bread crosswise into 4 equal pieces; cut each piece in half for sub-style sandwiches. Add 2 tablespoons butter to the reserved skillet. Once the butter stops foaming, toast half the bread, cut

side down, pressing and moving them to soak up all the butter, about 2 minutes. Transfer to a platter and brush with half the hot sauce. Repeat with the remaining butter, bread, and hot sauce.

4. Spread the cheese evenly on the bottoms of the bread. Layer the celery over the cheese. Thinly slice the chicken and place on the celery. Top with the watercress and finish by smearing the top pieces of bread with mayonnaise. Press the tops on the sandwiches and serve immediately or wrap and serve within 2 hours.

cook's note
TIPS
Here, we take a classic recipe for buffalo chicken wings, break it down into its individual parts, then rebuild it as a sandwich. There's usually a reason why certain combos taste good. Most of the time it's that the textures and flavors go well with each other. So here

you've got rich (cheese), creamy (cheese, mayo), crunchy (celery, watercress), cool (celery), and hot (sauce). Just like some people douse their wings in cheese and others live for hot sauce, everyone's preferences are different. Play around with texture and flavor to really make this sandwich your own.

soups

Homemade soup is awesome— it's a flexible one-pot meal that's healthy and soothing.

Makes you feel better—
even when you're not sick.

chicken "noodlette" soup
serves 6 • prep time: 30 minutes

1 medium carrot	2 tablespoons unsalted butter or extra-virgin olive oil	⅓ cup orzo or other tiny pasta (or broken-up spaghetti)
1 rib celery	¼ teaspoon kosher salt	½ rotisserie chicken (about 2½ cups cooked chicken)
¼ medium onion	4 cups low-sodium chicken broth (1 quart box or 2 small cans)	Handful fresh dill
1 clove garlic		Freshly ground black pepper

1. Peel the carrot. Slice the carrot, celery, and onion. Smash and peel the garlic.

 know-how 100, 99

2. Heat the butter in a large saucepan over medium heat, add all the vegetables, season with the salt, and cook until tender, about 8 minutes. Add the broth and bring to a boil over high heat. Add the pasta and cook uncovered until pasta is just tender, about 7 minutes.

3. Meanwhile, shred the chicken by hand or with 2 forks. Discard any tough stems from the dill. Chop the dill.

4. Add the chicken and simmer until heated through. Stir in the dill. Season with black pepper to taste.

upgrades
• Finely grate a lemon's zest and add it, along with a handful of freshly grated Parmesan cheese, to the soup.
• Or stir in a handful of torn spinach leaves or baby spinach at the end.
• Or make it curried: Add 1 tablespoon Madras curry powder to the butter. Substitute 1 cup cooked basmati rice (page 192) for the pasta. Stir in the juice of ½ a lime and a handful of chopped fresh cilantro instead of the cheese, lemon, and dill.

know-how 104

shopsmart
Low-sodium chicken broth in paper cartons is extremely convenient. It'll taste more like homemade if you add the rest of your rotisserie chicken (bones included), some garlic, some black peppercorns, and fresh parsley to your broth and simmer it for 30 to 60 minutes before straining. The leftovers freeze beautifully.

miso soup
serves 4 • prep time: 10 minutes

4   shiitake mushrooms
1   2-inch piece fresh ginger
4   cups chicken or mushroom
     broth or water (2 small cans or
     1 quart box)
2   cups baby spinach leaves or
     large spinach leaves, torn
     (optional)
8   ounces soft or silken tofu
2   scallions
¼   cup to ⅓ cup yellow or red
     miso paste
1   to 2 teaspoons soy sauce
1   to 2 teaspoons toasted sesame
     seeds or gomasio (optional)

1. Cut off and discard the stems from the shiitakes and thinly slice the caps. Thinly slice the ginger into coins with skin. Put the broth, ginger, and sliced shiitake mushrooms in a medium saucepan and simmer until the mushrooms are soft, about 3 minutes. Wash and add the spinach, if using, and cook until it wilts, about 1 minute.
▶ know-how 99

2. Meanwhile, cut the tofu into cubes, about ½ inch each. Thinly slice both the white and green parts of the scallions.
▶ know-how 99

3. Remove the broth from the heat and whisk in ¼ cup miso until smooth; taste, and add remaining miso, if necessary. Add the tofu and scallions. Season with the soy sauce and the sesame seeds, if using. Ladle the soup into warmed bowls and serve.

upgrades
Add grated carrots with the mushrooms, or use or a variety of mixed mushrooms.

miso wisdom
Miso paste comes in a few different colors, depending on the grain it's made from, which can be rice, barley, or soybean. Yellow miso is mellower and sweeter, and red miso is bolder and fuller flavored. Keep all miso in the fridge.

miso: yellow, red, and barley

TIPS
cook's note
Once you add the miso, don't let the soup boil. Intense heat changes the flavor of the miso.

shopsmart
• If you're having trouble finding these ingredients, check out an Asian market or a health food store. Either should have everything you need.

• Shiitake mushrooms have broad, flat caps and tough, woody stems. The stems are too chewy to eat, though they add lots of flavor when simmered in broth. If you can't find fresh, buy dried and soak them in hot water for half an hour before using.
• Gomasio is a combination of toasted sesame seeds and sea salt, sometimes with flakes of seaweed added. It's great on soup or sprinkled over rice.

hot & sour soup serves 4 • prep time: 20 minutes

1   4-inch piece fresh ginger
5   cups low-sodium chicken broth
      (about 3 small cans or
      1¼ 1-quart boxes)
½   package soft or firm tofu (about
      7 ounces)
3   scallions (white and green
      parts)
2   cups baby spinach leaves,
      or large leaves, torn (optional)
1   tablespoon soy sauce
      Generous pinch sugar
1   tablespoon plus 1 teaspoon rice
      or cider vinegar
      Lots of freshly ground black
      pepper
      Dark sesame oil (optional)

1. Thinly slice the ginger into 6 coins with skin. Bring the broth and the ginger to a boil in a large saucepan over high heat. Adjust the heat so the broth simmers and cook to lightly flavor with the ginger, about 5 minutes.

▶ know-how 99

2. Meanwhile, cut the tofu into small cubes. Thinly slice the scallions. Wash spinach, if using.

▶ know-how 99

3. Stir in the tofu, scallions, spinach, if using, and soy sauce. Cook until tofu is heated through and the spinach wilts, about 2 minutes more. Season with a pinch of sugar, the vinegar, and lots of black pepper. Serve drizzled with sesame oil, if desired.

upgrades
Add sliced mushrooms, grated carrots, or leftover chicken or pork with the scallions.

tofu: soft, firm, and silken

cook's note
TIPS Lots of different ingredients can contribute heat to food (fresh hot pepper, hot sauce, chile oils, crushed red pepper flakes). Here, it's freshly ground black pepper. See info on black pepper on page 12.

shopsmart
Tofu's low fat, high protein, really good for you, and tasty—give it a chance. Firm, soft, and silken tofu all come in individually wrapped blocks (usually found in the refrigerated section of the supermarket).

gazpacho serves 6 to 8 • prep time: 15 minutes

2	large ripe tomatoes (about 1½ pounds)
1	slightly heaping tablespoon kosher salt
1	small green bell pepper
1	medium cucumber
½	small red onion
1	clove garlic

3	cups low-sodium tomato/vegetable juice or tomato juice
3	tablespoons red or white wine vinegar or sherry vinegar
¼	cup extra-virgin olive oil
	Large handful fresh flat-leaf parsley leaves (about 1 cup)

½	bunch fresh mint leaves (about ½ cup)
	1 cup ice cubes
	Freshly ground black pepper
	Pinch sugar
	Dash hot pepper sauce
	Equipment: blender

1. Core and quarter the tomatoes; put them in a large bowl and sprinkle with half the salt. Stem, seed, and roughly chop the pepper. Peel, seed, and coarsely chop the cucumber. Chop the onion. Smash, peel, and slice the garlic. Add all the vegetables to the tomatoes and pour in the vegetable juice and vinegar.

▶ know-how 105, 101, 102, 99

2. Working in batches, puree the gazpacho base in a blender, filling it only about ½ full each time, and process to make a slightly coarse puree; pour into a serving bowl. With the last batch, while the motor is running, drizzle in the olive oil.

3. Chop the parsley and mint and stir into the soup. Stir in ice cubes. Chill the soup, covered, until cold, at least 1 hour. Season with the remaining salt, black pepper, sugar, and hot sauce to taste.

make it your own

• For a thicker gazpacho, stir in 1 or 2 tablespoons bread crumbs.
• Add a handful of fresh basil or dill instead of parsley and mint.

cook's note

TIPS We add the ice cubes to help quick-chill the gazpacho. As they melt, they also help dilute the gazpacho so it's not too thick.

shopsmart

Gazpacho tastes best in summer, when tomatoes are at their peak. Look for firm, fat, tomatoey-smelling tomatoes. And don't refrigerate them!

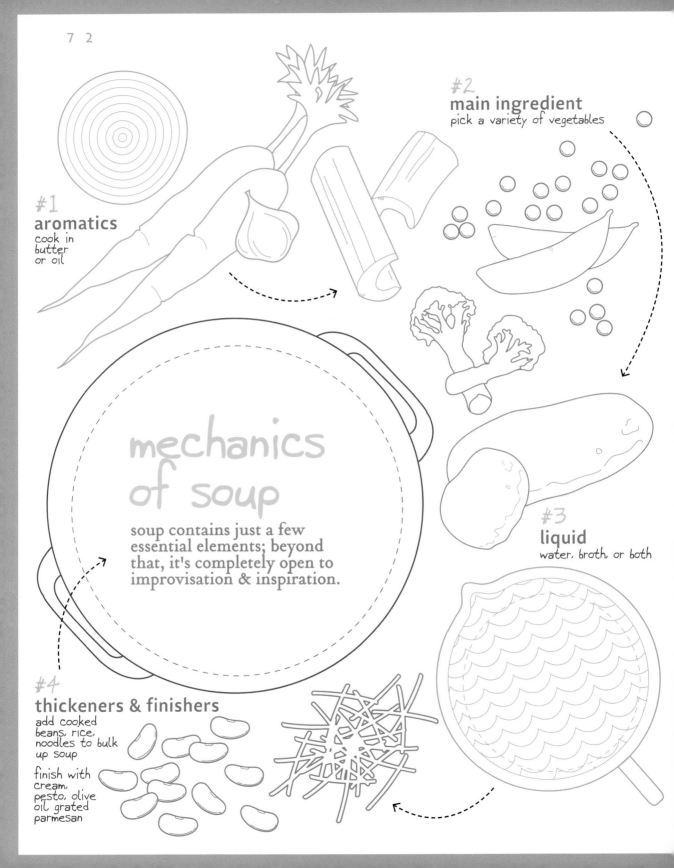

#1
aromatics
cook in
butter
or oil

#2
main ingredient
pick a variety of vegetables

mechanics
of soup

soup contains just a few
essential elements; beyond
that, it's completely open to
improvisation & inspiration.

#3
liquid
water, broth, or both

#4
thickeners & finishers
add cooked
beans, rice,
noodles to bulk
up soup

finish with
cream,
pesto, olive
oil grated
parmesan

the mechanics of soup
Or how to clean out your vegetable drawer in an hour and have something to show for it.

aromatics
onion, garlic, shallots, scallions, celery, carrots, fennel, or ginger
Sauté these in a little butter or oil. Or chop up some bacon and sauté the vegetables in the rendered fat. Or sauté ham or turkey bones in some butter or oil and cook the veggies in that.

main ingredient
Pick a vegetable, any vegetable, or pick a few. Starchy veggies mean thicker soups. Check the vegetable chart starting on page 209 for inspiration.

liquid
It wouldn't be soup otherwise, would it? Add water, broth, or both and simmer until everything's tender.

puree or not to puree?
After everything's cooked, you can puree it. The upside: creamy, fancy-looking. The downside: You'll have to wash the blender.

thickeners
Add cooked rice, noodles, beans, grains, or lentils to bulk up the soup and add texture.

finishers
Add a shot of cream, a swirl-in of pesto, a drizzle of extra-virgin olive oil, a sprinkling of freshly grated Parmesan, a fistful of cleaned spinach or chopped fresh herbs . . .

combos to try:
- carrots & parsnips
- potatoes & roasted peppers
- peas & bacon
- tomatoes & onions

creamless creamy vegetable soup serves 4 • prep time: 50 minutes

½ small onion or 2 shallots
3   russet potatoes or 1
     butternut squash (about
     2 pounds) or 2 10-ounce
     packages frozen squash
2   sprigs fresh thyme or pinch
     dried thyme
2   tablespoons unsalted butter
1½ teaspoons kosher salt, plus
     more for seasoning
5   cups water or low-sodium
     chicken broth (3 small cans or
     1-quart box plus 1 cup)
     Freshly ground black pepper
Equipment: blender or immersion blender

for serving:
¼ cup plain yogurt or sour cream
   (optional)
chives, chopped, for garnish
   (optional)

1. Thinly slice the onion. Peel and cut potatoes or squash into small bite-size chunks all about the same size. Strip the thyme leaves from the stems and discard the stems.

▶ know-how 99, 102, 103

2. Melt the butter in a large saucepan over low heat. Add the onion or shallot, thyme, and salt. Increase the heat to medium and cook, stirring occasionally, until the onion is tender, about 5 minutes. Add the potato or squash and water or broth. Bring to a boil, reduce the heat and simmer, uncovered, until the vegetables are totally tender, about 20 minutes.

3. Puree the soup in the pot with an immersion blender or in small batches in a blender (keep the lid cracked to allow steam to escape), until smooth. Return to the pot

and reheat. If using yogurt or sour cream, stir it in, but don't let the soup boil or it will curdle. Season with salt and black pepper to taste. Sprinkle with chives, if using, and serve warm.

upgrades
potato soup
Add a handful (about 2 ounces) of shredded cheddar cheese to the warm potato soup. Whisk until melted, then stir in about a cup defrosted frozen broccoli pieces.

squash soup
Add 1½ teaspoons curry powder to the onions while they are cooking. Scatter chopped cilantro over the finished soup.

either soup
• Stir in crumbled, cooked bacon (about 6 strips; see page 29 for how to cook it) and chopped chives right before serving.
• Instead of stirring the yogurt or sour cream into the soup, whisk it in a bowl to thin it out, then use a spoon to drizzle a free-form design on each serving of soup.

cook's note
TIPS If you don't have an immersion blender, be safe. Cool the soup for at least 5 minutes and transfer to a regular blender, filling no more than halfway. Don't seal the top. Lift one corner up a little to let the steam escape, put a kitchen towel on top, pulse a few times, then blend on high till smooth.

minute minestrone serves 4 to 6 • prep time: 15 minutes

2 medium zucchini (about 1 pound)
1 medium onion
3 garlic cloves
1 14.5-ounce can Great Northern, cannellini, or navy beans
¼ cup extra-virgin olive oil
2 teaspoons kosher salt, plus more for seasoning
   Freshly ground black pepper
1 14.5 ounce can diced tomatoes
3 to 4 cups low-sodium chicken broth (about 2 small cans or 1 quart box)
2 to 4 tablespoons prepared pesto or tapenade, such as olive, tomato, or artichoke

for serving:
freshly grated Parmesan cheese
Bruschetta (page 46) (optional)

1. Halve the zucchini lengthwise and cut crosswise into half-moon bite-size pieces. Halve and slice the onion. Peel and chop the garlic. Rinse and drain the beans.

know-how 99

2. Heat the olive oil in a large saucepan over medium heat. Add the onion and garlic; season with the 2 teaspoons salt and some black pepper; cook, stirring occasionally, until the onion wilts, about 5 minutes. Add the zucchini and tomatoes and cook until the tomatoes look dry, about 10 minutes. Add the beans and broth and adjust the heat so the soup simmers. Cook, uncovered, until the vegetables are tender, about 10 minutes more.

3. Just before serving, stir in the pesto and season with salt and black pepper to taste. Pour into warmed soup bowls and serve with grated cheese and Bruschetta, if desired.

make it your own

Soup recipes are incredibly forgiving of improvisation (they tend to reward it), and minestrone's a great place to practice—use any vegetables you've got in the house to make this soup your own. Add other vegetables: Sliced mushrooms, carrots, or yellow squash are all good, or check out the vegetable chart on pages 207-209 for ideas. Little noodles (like stars, tubes, broken spaghetti, whatever) also work. The noodles absorb the broth, so add about a cup more broth to keep it soupy.

salads

Fast, healthy, no-cook dishes that work perfectly as starters, mains, or sides.

salad wisdom

Our rule: The more salad you eat, the more dessert you deserve. Here's what you need to know to earn those sweets.

buy
- For convenience and ease, go with prewashed greens; they come either bagged or in a heap in the supermarket. Dig down into the heap for the perkiest greens.
- Need a break from bagged? Choose lettuce heads that are closed tight and have a little give when you squeeze them. If you see spots, pass. Buy bunch greens (like arugula or watercress) with roots attached (if you can), vibrant green leaves, and no wilting or yellowing.
- Think one handful of greens (small for a side, big for a main) per person, or two heads for a main-course salad for four.

store
- Go through the bag and ditch any less-than-perfect leaves when you get home (or trim any brown bruised edges from heads or bunches) to keep everything fresher longer. Keep them in a sealed plastic bag with a damp paper towel.
- Take rubber bands off of bunches; they stay better loose.

prep
- Speed up your prep: Have a big bowl of water at the ready to wash all of your greens at once.
- Use a knife or your fingers to get bite-size pieces. Grab bunches in both hands, stems in one hand, leaves in the other. Twist to rip off the stems and toss: stems in the garbage, leaves in the bowl of water.
- Swirl greens around the bowl of water, lift them all out to leave any grit behind, and dry them (get a salad spinner; they're great).

serve
- Always dress salad right before you serve it. You don't need tons of dressing, just enough to lightly coat each leaf.
- Toss lightly. Use your (clean!) hands so you know exactly how dressed the greens are. That's too weird? Then use tongs or big spoons.

green salad for one serves 1 (multiply for more) • prep time: 5 minutes or less

2 to 3 large handfuls prewashed mesclun or other salad greens, about 4 ounces

Extra-virgin olive oil
Vinegar (see notes on olive oil and vinegar, page 89)

Kosher salt and freshly ground black pepper

1. Even if the greens are prewashed, soak them in a big bowl of cold water for about 5 minutes. Lift them out of the water, leaving the grit behind, then put them in a salad spinner (don't pack them in or the greens will bruise) and spin dry. If you don't have a spinner, lay them on a clean towel and gently pat dry.

2. Put greens in a big bowl. Drizzle 3 teaspoons of olive oil (a regular teaspoon is fine; you don't need the measuring type) over the greens. Then drizzle with 1 teaspoon vinegar; season with salt and black pepper to your taste. Using tongs, 2 forks, big spoons, or your hands, toss just enough so all greens are lightly dressed. Eat from the bowl or transfer to a plate.

upgrades

Add crumbled cheese, sliced cucumbers, tomatoes, olives, bacon, fruit, or leftover chicken or steak.

salad wisdom

Add-ins like pasta, rice, leftover boiled potatoes, meat, cheese, or canned tuna all taste better when they're not fridge-cold, so leave them out for a few minutes while you get the salad together.

TIPS

don't panic
If the dressed greens are wilted and gloppy, there's probably too much dressing. Add an extra handful of greens and retoss.

pear & blue cheese salad serves 4 • prep time: 20 minutes

- ²/₃ cup nuts (walnuts, pecans, almonds, or cashews)
- 1 bunch watercress
- 1 bunch arugula
- 1 tablespoon cider vinegar

- 2 teaspoons whole-grain mustard
- ¼ teaspoon kosher salt, plus more to taste
- Freshly ground black pepper
- 3 tablespoons extra-virgin olive oil

- 1 Belgian endive
- 2 ripe pears, such as Anjou, Bartlett, or Comice
- 2 ounces mild blue cheese (about ½ cup loosely packed crumbles)

1. Preheat oven to 350°F. Spread the nuts on a rimmed baking pan in a single layer. Bake, shaking the pan occasionally, until the nuts are toasted and fragrant, 7 to 10 minutes. Let the nuts cool.

2. Trim the stems of the watercress and arugula. Wash and dry the leaves (see Step 1 of method on page 80).

3. Meanwhile, whisk the vinegar and mustard together in a large salad bowl. Season with the ¼ teaspoon salt and some black pepper. Gradually whisk in the olive oil, starting with a few drops and then adding the rest in a steady stream, to make a smooth, slightly thick dressing.

4. Halve the endive lengthwise, then thinly slice crosswise and add all the lettuces to the bowl. Quarter and core the unpeeled pears and thinly slice; add to the salad. Scatter the cheese and nuts over the salad, and season with salt and black pepper to taste. Toss the salad gently to evenly dress all the greens. Divide among 4 plates and serve immediately.

make it your own
Instead of pears with blue cheese, try apples with cheddar or grapes with Brie. Use 1½ cups halved seedless grapes with about 3 to 4 ounces firm Brie, cubed.

shopsmart
TIPS To tell if a pear is ripe, push the neck with your finger. If it gives way easily, it's ripe. (See our notes on buying fruit, page 20.) Any pear but the hard-as-rock brown kind works for this recipe.

cook's note
Strong cheese can take over a salad, so go easy unless you really like cheese. To crumble blue cheese without getting it all over your fingers, freeze it partially (just for 20 minutes or so), crumble it, and thaw the crumbles at room temperature while you make the rest of the salad.

shopsmart
If you're using Brie, look for a firmer one for this salad, one that's not totally runny so you can cut it easily—and yes, you can eat the rind.

italian celery salad serves 4 • prep time: 20 minutes

¼ medium red onion
½ bunch celery with leaves (about
   1 pound)
1 lemon
   Small handful fresh basil leaves
   (about ¼ cup)
½ teaspoon kosher salt
   Freshly ground black pepper
¼ cup extra-virgin olive oil
1- to 2-ounce wedge
   Parmigiano-Reggiano or grana-
   style hard grating cheese

1. Slice the onion as thinly as you can. Put in a bowl and cover with cold water.

▶ know-how 99

2. Peel tough, stringy fibers from celery ribs, if desired. Slice celery very thinly on an angle and chop leaves. Put ribs and leaves in a large bowl. Working over the bowl, grate zest off the lemon and then juice half of it. Roughly tear basil leaves and toss with other ingredients.

▶ know-how 100, 104

3. Drain and dry the onion and add to the salad. Season with the salt and a generous grinding of black pepper. Drizzle the olive oil over the salad and toss to coat evenly. Divide the salad among 4 serving plates. Use a vegetable peeler to shave large, thin strips of Parmigiano-Reggiano over each plate and serve immediately.

upgrades
Toss with diced turkey, ham, or salami. Don't have basil? Use fresh parsley or mint.

cook's note
TIPS Though you don't have to peel the celery, it'll make the texture better. Those tough, stringy outer fibers can be rough on the teeth.

lemony mushroom salad serves 4 to 6 • prep time: 20 minutes

½   lemon
2   tablespoons extra-virgin
     olive oil
1   teaspoon kosher salt, plus more
     to taste
     Freshly ground black pepper
10   ounces white or cremini
     mushrooms
1   scallion
     Handful fresh flat-leaf
     parsley leaves

1. Juice the lemon half into a medium bowl. Whisk in the oil, 1 teaspoon salt, and some black pepper. (Wrap the other lemon half up in plastic wrap and refrigerate; it'll keep for a couple of days.)

▶ know-how 104

2. Put the mushrooms in a colander and rinse quickly with cold water. Drain and pat dry. Trim off the stems and discard. Slice the mushrooms as thinly as you can and toss with the dressing. Marinate at room temperature for about 20 minutes.

3. Meanwhile, finely chop the white and green parts of the scallion. Chop the parsley. Toss the scallion and parsley with the mushrooms.

▶ know-how 99, 103

mushroom wisdom

Some chefs don't ever wash mushrooms, as they absorb water like sponges and can get soggy fast. Wash mushrooms for salad. If pan-frying, give them a good rubdown with a wet paper towel instead.

cleaning mushrooms

trimming a white mushroom

cremini & white mushrooms

TIPS

shopsmart

Pick mushrooms that have firm, spongy caps. Look at the cap's underside too—the whiter and tighter closed it is, the fresher. Avoid the ones that are wet, slippery, or have large black spots. Extend their life at home by taking them out of the plastic produce bags, wrapping them up in paper towels, and keeping them in the crisper. Cremini mushrooms are baby portobellos; they're supposed to be brown but should still be firm and spongy. Both cremini and white mushrooms are good raw; other mushrooms need cooking.

spicy carrot & garlic salad serves 4 to 6 • prep time: 20 minutes

1   lemon
1   ½-inch piece fresh ginger
1   tablespoon honey
1   teaspoon kosher salt
¼   teaspoon crushed red pepper
     flakes
     Pinch ground cinnamon
     Pinch ground cumin
3   tablespoons extra-virgin
     olive oil
1   pound medium carrots (about
     6 or 7 carrots)
1   clove garlic
¼   cup water
     Small handful fresh cilantro
     leaves

Equipment: microwave

1. Juice the lemon into a medium bowl. Peel and finely grate enough ginger to make 2 teaspoons and add to the lemon juice. Whisk in the honey, salt, red pepper flakes, cinnamon, and cumin. Gradually whisk in the olive oil, starting with a few drops and then adding the rest in a steady stream to make a smooth dressing.

know-how 104, 99

2. Peel and thinly slice the carrots into rounds. Smash, peel, and chop the garlic. Toss the carrots, garlic, and water in a medium microwave-safe bowl, cover tightly with plastic wrap, and microwave on HIGH for 3 minutes. Drain off any excess water.

know-how 100, 99

3. Pour the dressing over the hot carrots, toss, and let cool to room temperature. Coarsely chop the cilantro and stir into the salad.

whole carrots

shopsmart
TIPS Buy carrots that still have perky green tops—they're the freshest. Twist off the tops once you get them home to keep the carrots at their peak.

little tomato salad with fresh herbs

serves 4 • prep time: 20 minutes

1   pint (2 cups) ripe cherry or
    grape tomatoes
    Kosher salt and freshly ground
    black pepper
    Extra-virgin olive oil
    Small handful of fresh herbs,
    such as basil, flat-leaf parsley,
    mint, dill, or tarragon

Rinse and dry the tomatoes. Halve or quarter them, put them in a bowl, and season with some salt and black pepper. Drizzle with a couple tablespoons of olive oil, depending on the juiciness of the tomatoes. Remove herb leaves from stems and chop or tear leaves into pieces. Stir into the tomatoes. Serve immediately or set aside at room temperature for up to 2 hours. This salad can also serve as a juicy topping for chicken, fish, and burgers, or as an addition to greens.

▶ know-how 105, 103

soft-herb wisdom

• Choose vibrant green bunches of fresh basil, parsley, cilantro, and mint, with no yellowing or black leaves. Tarragon should have long, aromatic leaves with no black spots, and dill should have silky bright green fronds.

• Take off any rubber band holding the bunch together before you put the herbs away.

• If you've got roots attached to your herbs, put the roots into a shallow glass of water, then top the whole thing with a plastic bag to create a mini greenhouse in your fridge (see below).

• Wrap rootless herbs loosely in damp paper towels, put them into resealable plastic bags, and wash right before you use them.

storing basil

cook's note

TIPS Fresh herbs (as opposed to dried herbs in jars) are integral here; if you don't have any, this salad's equally good with just tomatoes, salt, black pepper, and extra-virgin olive oil.

choose your greens

Match mellow dressing with mellow greens and bold with bold:
Boston lettuce with mint and lemon juice, arugula with balsamic
vinegar and red onion, and watercress with blue cheese.

arugula

watercress

baby spinach

radicchio

romaine

green or red leaf

boston lettuce

salad untossed: greens, oils & vinegars

greens

- red leaf lettuce is mild tasting (that is, not too lettuce-y), with crisp, ruffly red leaves.
- boston lettuce (sometimes called butter lettuce) has tender, soft leaves and a buttery flavor. Mix it up with crunchier greens for a salad or serve it alongside lighter main dishes.
- romaine is the classic Caesar-salad lettuce. It's hearty, crunchy, and lasts a long time in the fridge.
- baby spinach is tender and delicate, and is equally good raw or cooked.
- arugula is sharp and tangy, with sturdy leaves and snappy stems.
- watercress, a member of the mustard family, has a nice crunch and a peppery bite.
- radicchio's deep red leaves are firm, crisp, and a little bitter—mix it up with sweeter greens.
- meslcun is a mixture of young greens, usually on the tender and mild side.

oils & vinegars

- The simplest dressing is 3 to 4 parts oil to 1 part vinegar.
- Mild-tasting oil needs less vinegar; strong oil needs more.
- Extra-virgin olive oil (the most olivey-tasting kind) has a full-bodied flavor: usually peppery, fruity, grassy, or flowery.
- Buy by color, not by price: Bright green oils are peppery and a little bitter, and yellow oils are warmer and butterier.
- Keep olive oil in an airtight container in a cool, dark place (not the fridge).
- Nut and seed oils have a rich, toasty flavor perfect for strong greens or Asian food. Keep them in the fridge.
- Start small—buy little bottles until you figure out what you like.
- Any vinegar is good for salads except for distilled white vinegar (too harsh). Every kind of vinegar tastes a little different: Balsamic is sweet, cider vinegar is fruity, and rice vinegar is mellow.
- Or try freshly squeezed lemon, lime, or grapefruit juice instead of vinegar.
- Like your dressings creamy? Check out the three dressings on page 91.

extra-virgin olive oils

homemade salad dressings
each recipe makes about 1 cup • prep time: 5 minutes

These dressings are tasty and versatile. Use the mustard dressing on potatoes, rinsed canned beans, or orzo pasta. Drizzle the ranch on your sandwiches. Toss the spicy miso dressing with leftover chicken for low fat high flavor chicken salad.

mustard dressing

1	tablespoon Dijon-style or whole-grain mustard
¼	cup white or red wine vinegar
2	teaspoons kosher salt
	Freshly ground black pepper
⅔	to ¾ cup extra-virgin olive oil

Whisk the mustard, vinegar, salt, and some black pepper in a small bowl. Gradually whisk in the oil, starting with a few drops and then adding the rest in a steady stream, to make a smooth, slightly thick dressing. Use now or refrigerate in a tightly sealed container for up to 3 days.

upgrades
· Add minced red onion, shallot, or scallion.
· Add a couple tablespoons of chopped fresh herbs, such as basil, parsley, or thyme.
· Substitute nut oil for some of the olive oil.

shopsmart
TIPS French-style Dijon mustard is pale, strong, and sharp-tasting. If you like, experiment with other mustards—such as the mellower whole-seed kind. Save the ballpark stuff for hot dogs, though.

ranch dressing

1	scallion (white and green parts)
1	small or ½ medium clove garlic
1	cup mayonnaise
⅓	cup buttermilk
1	teaspoon white wine vinegar
½	teaspoon kosher salt
2	tablespoons fresh flat-leaf parsley
	Freshly ground black pepper

Equipment: blender

1. Roughly chop the scallion. Smash and peel the garlic. Put the scallion and garlic into the blender and process until the garlic pieces stop bouncing around. Add the mayonnaise, buttermilk, vinegar, and salt and process until just blended. Transfer to a bowl.

▶ know-how 99

2. Chop the parsley and stir into the dressing. Add black pepper to taste. Use now or refrigerate in a tightly sealed container for up to 3 days.

▶ know-how 103

upgrades
· Add ½ of a chipotle pepper (from canned chipotles en adobo).
· Add ¼ cup finely chopped fresh dill.
· Add fresh orange or lemon zest.

sriracha-miso dressing

1	1-inch piece fresh ginger
3	tablespoons yellow (shiro) miso
2	tablespoons water
1	tablespoon rice vinegar (not the seasoned kind)
1	teaspoon soy sauce
½	teaspoon Asian chile paste, such as Sriracha or sambal oelek
½	cup peanut oil

Equipment: blender

Peel the ginger. Drop the ginger into the blender and process until finely chopped. Add the miso, water, vinegar, soy sauce, and chile paste; puree. With the blender running, drizzle in the peanut oil to make a smooth, slightly thick dressing. Serve or refrigerate in a tightly sealed container for up to 3 days.

▶ know-how 99

shopsmart
TIPS · Asian chile pastes generally can be found in jars in the international aisle of your grocery store. Keep them in the fridge and they'll last forever, as a little goes a long way.
· See our notes on miso on page 68.

quicky cobb salad serves 4 to 6 • prep time: 20 minutes

3   slices bacon
1   ripe Hass avocado
2   ripe medium tomatoes
2   hard-boiled eggs (page 25)
     Kosher salt and freshly ground
       black pepper
8   cups mesclun salad greens
     (about 7 ounces)
2   cups shredded cooked chicken
     (about ½ of a rotisserie chicken)
2   ounces mild blue cheese (about
     ½ cup loosely packed
     crumbles)
3   tablespoons extra-virgin
     olive oil
1   tablespoon red wine vinegar

1. Cut bacon in half crosswise. Spread out on a paper towel on a microwave-safe plate and cover with another piece of paper towel. Microwave on high until crisp, 3 to 4 minutes. Cool. (Or, see cooking instructions on page 29.)

2. Halve, seed, and dice the avocado. Core and dice the tomatoes. Peel and chop the hard-boiled eggs. Layer the avocado, tomato, and eggs in a large salad bowl, seasoning with salt and black pepper as you go.

▶ know-how 106, 105

3. Top with the mesclun greens, then scatter the chicken and cheese on top. Crumble the bacon over the salad. Season again with salt and black pepper. At the table, drizzle with the oil and vinegar and toss until the salad is evenly dressed.

hard-boiled egg

TIPS

a side of history
This salad got its start as a midnight snack when Hollywood restaurateur Bob Cobb got hungry one night in 1937 and raided the fridge. Raid your own fridge for this one—it's flexible. Add cooked potato or leftover roast turkey, or if you've got homemade dressing (see page 91), use that. Or hit up the grocery store salad bar for grilled chicken, chopped eggs, or precut vegetables.

cook's note
If you pack this to go, put the dressing in a separate container and keep the avocado whole. Slice the avocado and toss it all together when you're ready to eat.

shrimp salad with mango & lime
serves 4 to 6 • prep time: 20 minutes

½ small red onion
1 small clove garlic
2 teaspoons kosher salt, plus
more as needed
2 limes
½ teaspoon chili powder
¼ cup extra-virgin olive oil
1¼ pounds cooked, peeled
medium shrimp
1 ripe mango
1 14-ounce can black beans
1 head romaine lettuce or
3 romaine hearts
Large handful fresh cilantro
leaves

1. Thinly slice the onion and soak in cold water (to mellow the bite) while you prepare the rest of the salad.
▶ know-how 99

2. Smash and peel the garlic clove, sprinkle with a pinch of salt, and, with the flat side of a large knife, mash and smear the mixture to a coarse paste. Transfer to a large serving bowl. Juice the limes into the bowl. Add the 2 teaspoons salt and the chili powder. Gradually whisk in the olive oil, starting with a few drops and then adding the rest in a steady stream to make a dressing. Toss shrimp in dressing.
▶ know-how 99, 104

3. Peel and dice the mango. Add to the bowl.
▶ know-how 105

4. Rinse and drain the beans in a colander and add to the bowl. Tear the romaine and cilantro into bite-size pieces, rinse, dry, and add to the bowl. Drain and dry the onion and scatter over the salad. Gently toss the salad together and serve.

upgrades
Add 1 diced red bell pepper, 1 cup cherry tomatoes, or a diced avocado.

bean wisdom
Canned beans are super-convenient, but need a quick rinse (in a colander, with cold water) before use.

TIPS

shopsmart
• Good mangoes have soft, firm skin and a sweet smell. They're generally sold slightly unripe and will ripen on their own at home if kept at room temperature.
• Look for ready-to-go cocktail shrimp at the fish counter (check the deli counter too).

southeast asian-style beef salad
serves 4 (10 cups) • prep time: 20 minutes

12	ounces flank steak (about half of a full one)	
¾	cup Sriracha-Miso Dressing (page 91) or storebought ginger-miso dressing	
3	scallions	

1	medium carrot
1	Kirby cucumber
1	to 2 bird's eye chiles or 1 jalapeño
1	bunch fresh cilantro or mint
1	lime

1	head red leaf or 2 heads Boston or Bibb or 10-ounce bag prewashed salad greens, preferably an Asian mix
1	cup mung bean sprouts (optional)
1	large handful roasted peanuts or cashews (about ½ cup)

1. Brush the steak with about ¼ cup of the miso dressing. Marinate at room temperature for up to an hour or cook immediately. When ready to cook, position a broiler pan on the rack closest to the broiler and preheat to high.

2. Carefully lay the steak in the center of the hot pan and broil until the steak is browned but still tender to the touch, about 4 minutes. Turn the steak and broil

another 2 to 3 minutes for medium rare (an instant-read thermometer inserted sideways into the steak will register about 130°F). Transfer the steak to a cutting board to rest for 5 to 10 minutes.

3. Thinly slice the white and green parts of the scallions. Peel the carrot. Thinly slice the cucumber, carrot, and chiles. Tear off and discard any tough stems from the cilantro; wash and dry the leaves. Cut the lime into thin wedges.

▶ know-how 99, 102, 100, 103

4. Wash and dry the lettuce. Arrange on a large platter or individual serving plates, along with the vegetables, sprouts, if using, nuts, chiles, and cilantro. Thinly slice the steak against the grain (see page 163) and add to the platter. Garnish with the lime wedges. Serve, passing the remaining dressing at the table.

make it your own
Serve this with big lettuce leaves and extra dressing alongside and have your guests make their own lettuce wraps.

thai bird's eye chile & mung bean sprouts

TIPS

shopsmart
• Asian-labeled mixed greens tend to have tangy, sharp add-ins like mizuna and tatsoi, which add mustardy zip to salads. If you can't find them, look for baby spinach or arugula.

• Kirby cucumbers are small and thin-skinned (they look like fresh pickles).
• Bird's eye chiles, sometimes called piri-piri, are small, fiery chiles sold both fresh and dried. (See page 40 for our note on using chiles.)

serrated knife
Its rippled edge is perfect for slicing bread, cheese, or tomatoes or chopping chocolate. The longer the blade, the more power and control you'll have. In a pinch, a steak knife can stand in.

paring knife
For little jobs: coring apples or tomatoes or trimming vegetables. It should be lightweight, with a 2- to 4- inch blade.

chef's knife
Use this for all your major slicing, dicing, and chopping. The blade is wide, between 6 to 10 inches long, and curved; the handle should feel solid and weighty.

know-how

What you need to know to make the food you want to eat.

Hold the knife in a relaxed grip; choke up on the handle, with your thumb and index finger just touching the blade for balance.

the basics on
how to hold a knife

A sharp knife, used properly, makes everything easier (and safer). Cut away from yourself on a cutting board—not into your hand. Be aware at all times where your knife is and where your fingers are in relationship to it. Use a sharpening steel regularly (see foodnetwork. com for a video demo) and get your knives sharpened twice a year at your local cookware store.

how to buy a knife

Good knives last decades, so make sure yours are right for you. Your knife should feel comfortable in your hand; try it out at the store to make sure. Once you have good knives, keep them sharp. Store them in a block or on a magnet, never in a drawer. Don't put them in the dishwasher—it'll damage the blades.

Move the knife in a rocking motion from front to back, keeping the edge in contact with the board. Cut as you move the blade forward.

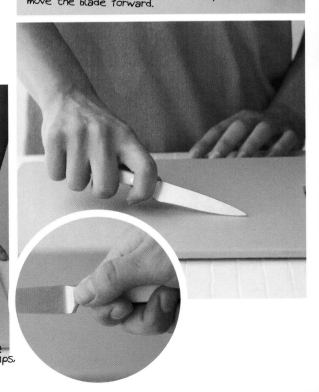

Keep your fingertips tucked under your knuckles (like a claw) away from the blade. If you can see your fingertips, so can the knife; keep them tucked.

garlic

the basics of
aromatics

circular smushing motion

garlic
Separate cloves by pushing down on the head. Smash cloves with the flat side of your chef's knife to loosen peels. Mince with a rocking motion. To make fine paste, sprinkle minced garlic with salt and use the wide side of the knife to smush.

onion

scallion

ginger

chiles

onions
Cut off pointy end. Cut in half through root. Peel off papery skin. Place cut side on board. Slice crosswise for slices or quarter for chunks. To chop, make a grid of horizontal and vertical cuts, leaving root end intact, then slice across front. For scallions, pull off discolored outer layers and trim root end.

ginger
Peel with bowl of a spoon or a peeler. Slice crosswise for coins. To mince, use a fine-mesh grater.

chiles
Slice in half lengthwise. Remove seeds with tip of paring knife. Trim stem. A chile's natural oils burn; don't rub your eyes when working with chiles, and always wash hands after handling.

the basics of •
prepping vegetables

How you cut a vegetable affects both how it cooks and how the finished dish turns out. The smaller the cut, the less time it'll take to cook and the more you'll taste of it in each bite. Slices are great for stir-fries; chunks stand up to stewing and roasting.

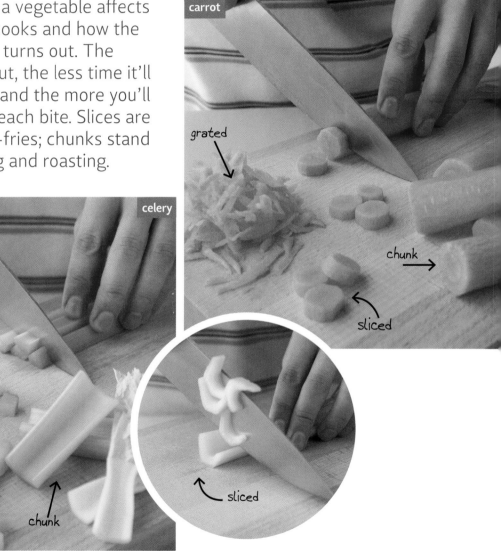

carrot

grated

chunk

sliced

celery

diced

chunk

sliced

bell pepper

broccoli

fennel

carrot

Peel, then cut off top and bottom. If grating, use a box grater, rotating the carrot (like sharpening a pencil).

celery

Peel if necessary (see page 84), then slice. Use the leaves!

bell peppers: red, yellow, or green

Cut the pepper's sides off. Discard the stem and seeds. Place skin side down on cutting board and cut into strips and then crosswise for diced, as needed.

broccoli

Cut florets from stalk and cut into desired size. Peel and slice stalk.

fennel

Trim fronds. Halve through the root. Cut out core, if desired (leave it in if roasting). Slice or wedge. Cut slices crosswise for diced.

TIPS

veggie-cutting wisdom
Always make sure whatever you're cutting is safely grounded on the board. If there isn't a flat side, make one by slicing off a thin piece from the bottom.

the basics of.
prepping vegetables

squash

cucumber

squash
Trim bottom. Cut in half; scoop out
seeds with a spoon. You don't have
to peel them if you don't want to.

cucumber
Slice into half-moons or peel and
seed with a spoon.

TIPS cucumber wisdom
Kirby cucumbers (smaller, thin-skinned, lumpy) and
English cucumbers (long, dark green, wrapped in
plastic) don't need to be peeled or seeded. Regular
cucumbers, since they're waxed, need to be peeled or
washed; seeding is optional.

handful

stripping

bruising

crumbling

bouquet garni

the basics of
using herbs

Fresh herbs bring lots of flavor to even the simplest dish. If you can't find or don't like a particular herb, feel free to use another, adding to taste. Easy swaps: basil with mint or dill, parsley with cilantro, or rosemary with thyme.

handful
Whether using a handful or a pinch, there's no need to be super-exact with herbs.

stripping
For woody herbs like thyme or rosemary, pull leaves from stems with your fingertips, against the direction they grow. Or add whole sprigs to sauces or stews, removing them before serving. For parsley or cilantro, shave the leaves off the stems with a sharp chef's knife.

bruising
Turn your knife over and lightly pound herbs to release flavors.

crumbling
You can substitute dried herbs for fresh in long-cooked dishes like stews. Use $1/3$ the amount of fresh herbs called for in the recipe and crumble them between your fingers for best flavor.

bouquet garni
Parsley, thyme, and bay leaf tied together with kitchen string or unwaxed dental floss. Use in stews.

the basics of
prepping fruit

Anything with seeds in it—even tomatoes and avocados—is considered a fruit. Some need to be peeled and seeded, others just need to be peeled.

peeling & slicing citrus

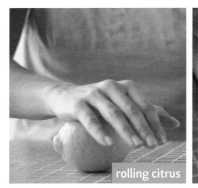
rolling citrus

juicing citrus

rolling citrus
For the most juice, roll citrus under the palm of your hand on the counter before squeezing.

juicing citrus
Use a citrus reamer (or a fork) to get the juice out or squeeze by hand.

peeling & slicing citrus
Cut off the tops and bottoms. Then cut off the skin and white pith, following the curve of the fruit, halve (if desired), and slice.

zesting citrus
Grate the zest (the colored outside of the skin) on a fine grater or rasp. Rotate the fruit and zest different spots to avoid the white pith. For larger strips, use a vegetable peeler.

zesting citrus

citrus-fruit wisdom
TIPS The white part between the zest and the fruit is called pith, and it's bitter. When you're peeling or zesting a citrus, avoid it (or cut it away).

the basics of
baking skills

Good technique is the
first step to good results.

room-temp eggs

separating egg

cracking an egg

vanilla bean

cracking an egg
Gently tap an egg against a flat
surface, then separate the two
halves of shell.

room-temp eggs
Quickly bring eggs to room
temperature by immersing them in
warm water for 5 minutes.

separating egg
Over a bowl, either use the shells
to pour the yolk back and forth

between the shell halves; or use
clean hands: Hold the yolk and let
the white drip down.

vanilla bean
Split in half lengthwise, then
scrape out the seeds. Use seeds in
your recipes; store pod in sugar or
vodka for homemade infusions.

cake test

cake test
Cake is done when it starts pulling
away from the sides of the pan and
a toothpick inserted in the center
comes out clean.

TIPS

vanilla bean wisdom
Vanilla beans are expensive but delicious. Good-
quality pure vanilla extract can be substituted in
most baking recipes.

liquid measure

the basics of
measuring

Exact measuring is key to getting good results when baking. You'll need three types of measuring equipment: a glass or plastic measuring cup with a spout for wet ingredients, a set of scoop-shape cups in graduated sizes for dry ingredients, and a set of measuring spoons. Don't use a measuring cup intended for wet ingredients for dry ingredients.

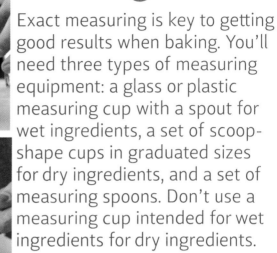

dry measure

brown sugar

liquid measure
Check your measuring cup on the counter at eye level to make sure you're measuring accurately.

dry measure
Lightly spoon the flour or sugar into the cup, then run a knife along the edge to level it off.

brown sugar
Firmly press brown sugar into the measuring cup.

season to taste
Season to taste means look for the right balance of sweet, sour, bitter, salty, and umami (see an explanation of umami on page 155). Adding salt makes flavors brighter, enhancing what's already there. You don't want your food to taste salty; you want it to taste like itself. So when we tell you to season to taste, it means add as much salt and black pepper as you need to make food taste right to you. Everyone's palate is different; add as you see fit.

When you're not baking, it's fine to estimate amounts for things like herbs, salt, or grated cheese; try to get a feel for what a tablespoon feels like in your hand.

the basics of
prepping fruit

avocado

Slice the avocado in half, then twist to separate the halves. Carefully whack the pit with your knife; twist to lift pit out. For diced avocado, make crosshatch cuts just down to the skin. Scoop flesh out with spoon.

avocado

tomato

mango

pomegranate

tomato

Cut out the small circle at the top (the core) with your paring knife, then slice or dice with a serrated knife.

mango

Cut top and bottom off so it stands up. Cut away skin with a paring knife. Cut off wide, flat sides (avoiding the pit in the middle), then cut off narrow edges.

pomegranate

Break in half and use a wooden spoon to knock out the seeds. Discard the white pith.

whipped cream

chopping chocolate

prepping a pan

trim to make pan-size circle

whipping cream

Use an ice-cold bowl and a large whisk to whip cream fastest. Don't overwhip it; it should look silky and creamy, not curdy.

chopping chocolate

Use a serrated knife to chop chocolate finely for sauce and garnish.

prepping a pan: first, butter

Rub or brush butter or oil gently over the surface of the pan.

then, paper

Fold a square of parchment into quarters, then fold into a triangle. Place tip in center of pan. Cut away excess paper to make a pan-size circle. Lightly butter paper.

then, flour

Toss flour into the pan, then tilt and twist pan so all surfaces are lightly covered, then tap the pan on the countertop to get rid of excess flour.

For video demos of everything here and more, check out foodnetwork.com

noodles

The go-with-anything comfort food that can be dressed up or down for any occasion.

noodle wisdom

Noodles can come from all over the world, not just Italy. To get noodles on the table, all you need to do is boil water. To get perfect noodles on the table:

choose
- Different noodle shapes do actually taste different. The general rule of thumb for Italian pasta (usually made from wheat) is this: The thinner the sauce, the thinner the noodle, and the chunkier the sauce, the fatter and more tubelike the noodle (the better to trap bits of sauce). So spaghetti is great with oil, and penne's better for chunky marinara sauce.
- Asian-style noodles can be made from rice, wheat, or bean flour. Rice noodles are delicate and quick cooking; wheat noodles are hearty and chewy. Bean noodles (also called cellophane noodles) are superlight and springy.
- Couscous (think of it as a mini noodle) comes from the Middle East. It's made from semolina flour and is fine-grained and crumbly.

cook
- Give it room. Use a big pot (at least 6 quarts) and about 4 quarts of water per pound for Italian- or Asian-style noodles.
- The water should be salty (use at least a tablespoonful of salt per pound of noodles) and don't add oil; it makes the sauce slide off and makes it hard to clean the pot.
- Stir the noodles frequently to prevent clumping. Cook them uncovered at a rapid boil (if the water's not boiling, put a slightly ajar lid on the pot) until done.

check
- The only way to tell that noodles are done is by tasting them, not throwing or dropping or stretching or pulling or any of those things.
- "Al dente" means "to the tooth" in Italian. Perfectly cooked noodles shouldn't be crunchy but should have just a little bit of firmness to them. See the picture on page 124 for guidance. When they're done, drain them immediately in a colander. Don't rinse them unless the recipe calls for it, and you don't have to shake them bone-dry—a little water is good. Save a cupful of the cooking water before you drain the noodles; if the final dish looks dry or the sauce is too thick, add the water.

serve
- Noodles wait for no one. The second they're done, toss them with butter, oil, or sauce to coat, adding more sauce until they're as saucy as you want them.
- As soon as the noodles are sauced, seasoned, and cheesed (if called for), get them served and eaten.

spaghetti with olive oil & garlic serves 4 to 6 • prep time: 15 minutes

1   teaspoon kosher salt, plus more
      for pasta-cooking water and
      to taste
1   pound spaghetti
4   to 6 cloves garlic
½   cup extra-virgin olive oil
      Freshly ground black pepper
      Small handful fresh flat-leaf
      parsley leaves
      Chunk of Parmesan cheese

1. Bring a large pot of cold water to a boil over high heat and salt it generously. Add the spaghetti and boil, stirring occasionally, until al dente, about 12 minutes.

2. Meanwhile, make the sauce. Smash, peel, and coarsely chop the garlic. In a large skillet combine the garlic, olive oil, 1 teaspoon salt, and some black pepper. Warm the garlic and oil over low heat, stirring occasionally, until the garlic turns golden; be careful not to let the oil get too hot or the garlic will turn brown and bitter.

▶ know-how 99

3. Chop the parsley. When the pasta is just done, use tongs to lift it out of the water, letting most of the water drip off. Carefully transfer the pasta to the skillet. Stir and turn the pasta with tongs to coat all the strands with the garlic. If the noodles seem dry, add up to ¼ cup of the pasta-cooking water. Season to taste with salt and black pepper. Transfer to a large serving bowl and mix in the parsley. Serve with freshly grated Parmesan.

▶ know-how 103

upgrades

· Add a pinch of crushed red pepper flakes to the oil.
· Toss in other fresh herbs like chopped basil or oregano.
· Wilt a couple handfuls of spinach in the oil before adding the pasta.
· Add chopped broccoli to the oil before the pasta.
· Add 1 to 1½ cups chopped greens (such as kale, broccoli rabe, or escarole) to the pasta water after removing the spaghetti and cook (about 30 seconds for kale or escarole or 2 minutes for broccoli rabe). Drain, squeezing out excess water; add to spaghetti and sauce.

garlic wisdom

First things first: The fist-size white-paper-covered thing you buy in the store is a head of garlic. Break that into pieces and you have cloves. Buy clean, dry heads of garlic with no brown patches (on the outside) or green sprouts (coming out the top), though purple-tinged white outside is extra good. Keep unpeeled garlic at room temperature in a dark place and it'll last a long time. See page 99 for how to peel and chop it.

head of garlic & 1 clove

romano and parmesan cheeses

TIPS

shopsmart

There are few better-tasting things in the world than really, really good Parmesan (or Parmigiano-Reggiano when it comes from a certain region of Italy). It's nutty, sharp, crumbly, salty, delicious, and expensive. It's really good shaved over salad, grated over pasta, or chunked up and eaten with your fingers. But if you're not ready to take the plunge, a chunk of grana-style cheese, such as Grana Padano, is a great place to start. Granas are hard, grainy cheeses that add well-rounded Parmy flavor to everything you grate them into. Or try sheep's milk pecorino Romano cheese—it's like grana but more tangy and less nutty. But be sure it's freshly grated—it really makes a world of difference.

penne with pesto serves 4 • prep time: 15 minutes

1 large bunch fresh basil
2 cloves garlic
¼ cup pine nuts
½ cup extra-virgin olive oil
½ cup freshly grated
  Parmesan cheese
½ teaspoon kosher salt, plus more
  for pasta-cooking water and
  to taste
  Freshly ground black pepper
1 pound penne rigate or other
  ridged small-tube pasta

Equipment: food processor

1. Pluck the basil leaves from the stems (you should have about 2 cups leaves). Wash the leaves in a large bowl of cold water and dry in a salad spinner or gently pat dry with paper towels. Smash and peel the garlic.

▶ know-how 99

2. Put the basil, garlic, and pine nuts in a food processor and pulse until coarsely chopped. With the food processor running, gradually add the olive oil and process until the pesto is smooth. Transfer the pesto to a large bowl and stir in the cheese. Season pesto with the ½ teaspoon salt and some black pepper to taste.

3. Bring a large pot of cold water to a boil over high heat and salt it generously. Add the penne and boil, stirring occasionally, until al dente, 8 to 10 minutes. Drain in a colander, saving about ¼ cup pasta-cooking water. Add the pasta to the bowl. Use tongs and toss with enough of the cooking water so the pesto coats the pasta evenly. Season with salt and black pepper to taste.

upgrades

• Top dressed pesto pasta with ½ pound chopped fresh mozzarella balls (bocconcini), 3 ripe medium tomatoes cut in large chunks, and ½ cup pitted, roughly chopped black olives (we like kalamata).
• Or add 1 to 2 cups cooked chicken or shrimp.

make it your own

• Instead of basil in the pesto, try 1 cup parsley, 1 cup fresh spinach leaves, 2 tablespoons fresh rosemary leaves, and 2 tablespoons fresh thyme leaves. Substitute walnuts for pine nuts.
• Add ¼ cup ricotta cheese when processing basil, garlic, and pine nuts for a creamy pesto that's great with tortellini or ravioli.

TIPS

cook's note
Put a piece of plastic wrap directly on the surface of the pesto, and store it in the fridge for up to a week. Or, freeze it for up to 3 months; for optimum flavor and texture, add the cheese after thawing and before serving.

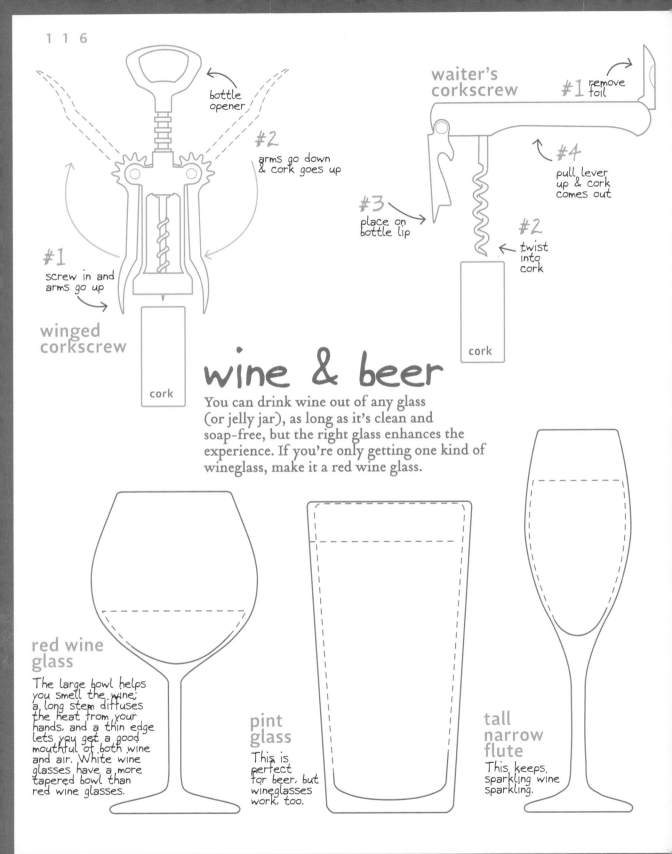

bottle opener

winged corkscrew

#1
screw in and arms go up

#2
arms go down & cork goes up

cork

waiter's corkscrew

#1 remove foil

#4
pull lever up & cork comes out

#3
place on bottle lip

#2
twist into cork

cork

wine & beer

You can drink wine out of any glass (or jelly jar), as long as it's clean and soap-free, but the right glass enhances the experience. If you're only getting one kind of wineglass, make it a red wine glass.

red wine glass

The large bowl helps you smell the wine; a long stem diffuses the heat from your hands, and a thin edge lets you get a good mouthful of both wine and air. White wine glasses have a more tapered bowl than red wine glasses.

pint glass

This is perfect for beer, but wineglasses work, too.

tall narrow flute

This keeps sparkling wine sparkling.

want wine with that?

Forget everything you've heard about red with meat, white with fish. The best wine to serve with anything is whatever you feel comfortable drinking with it. Wine shouldn't be scary; it's about enjoyment. That said, try to match the flavors in the drink to the flavors in your dish. If there's wine or beer in the main dish, serve similar-tasting wine or beer with the meal.

Drink-and-food matching is kind of like pizza: Even when it's bad, it's still pretty good—and when it's good, it's amazing. Here's a drop-in-a-bucket's worth of guidelines, but it's always best to ask someone. The wine specialist at your store will be happy to help you, or check out our website, foodnetwork.com, for more details.

- **meat & potatoes**
  Big, red, and fruity, like American red Zinfandel or Australian Shiraz. Or dark beer like stout, bock, or porter.
- **red sauce & garlic**
  Herby and mouth-gripping: Chianti Classico, Barbaresco, or Rioja.
- **chiles & cilantro**
  Mellow, full whites or spicy reds: South African Chardonnay, Spanish Rosado, South American Malbec or Merlot, or Mexican lager beer.
- **big roasts or flavorful fish**
  Assertive, fruity white or mellow red: California Chardonnay, French whites from the Rhône, Pinot Noir, or Pilsner beer.
- **ginger & spice**
  A little sweet (in a good way, with an edge): German or New York Riesling, Austrian Gewürztraminer, or wheat beer.

- **salads, vegetables & unassuming fish**
  Crisp, acidic: New Zealand Sauvignon Blanc or white wines from the Loire Valley.
- **when in doubt**
  Champagne. Goes with everything (including fried chicken, sushi, popcorn, and soup). Prosecco, Cava, Sekt, and sparkling wine are all Champagne-like wine not made in the Champagne region of France. They work, too.

cooking with wine & beer

The rule of thumb is always to cook with something that you'd drink (though you shouldn't spend a lot). Stuff labeled "cooking wine" is rarely the best option. Most wine stores have discount bottles you can buy and keep for cooking. As far as beer goes, cook with beer that tastes like something.

TIPS

cook's note
Wine lasts for about 4 days after you open it. Get a "clamshell" stopper for Champagne; stick the cork back in (or screw the top back on) regular wine and keep it in the fridge. Let reds come to room temperature before serving.

fusilli with tomatoes & basil serves 6 • prep time: 20 minutes

1   pound fusilli pasta (corkscrews)
4   to 5 ripe medium tomatoes (about 2 pounds)
1½ teaspoons kosher salt, plus more for pasta-cooking water and to taste
   Freshly ground black pepper
1   large clove garlic
½   cup extra-virgin olive oil
1   tablespoon white wine vinegar
   Large handful fresh basil leaves (a heaping ¾ cup)
2   to 4 ounces grated or shredded Parmesan cheese or ricotta salata, for serving (optional)

1. Bring a large pot of cold water to a boil over high heat and salt it generously. Add the pasta and boil, stirring occasionally, until al dente, about 10 minutes.

2. Meanwhile, core and dice the tomatoes and put in a large serving bowl. Season with 1¼ teaspoons of the salt and some black pepper. Smash and peel the garlic clove, sprinkle with the remaining ¼ teaspoon salt, and, with the flat side of a large knife, mash and smear the mixture to a coarse paste. Add the garlic paste, olive oil, and vinegar to the tomatoes. Rinse the basil leaves and pat dry. Tear into pieces and add to the tomatoes. (You can make the tomato mixture up to 2 hours ahead—but don't refrigerate.)

know-how 105, 99

3. When the pasta is ready, drain well and add to the bowl. Season with salt and black pepper to taste and toss to coat evenly. Serve, with the cheese if desired, immediately or at room temperature.

upgrades

Add pitted black olives, diced fresh mozzarella, or both. Or add finely diced soaked red onion or minced shallots.

fresh-tomato wisdom

• When you're thinking uncooked tomato sauce, the taste of the tomato is key. If it's the middle of summer, get whatever smells and tastes best at the store or farmer's market (or from the garden) or a mix of varieties for color and flavor.
• Though all tomatoes taste best in the summer, there are a few main tomato types to look for in the off-season: Roma tomatoes (sometimes called plum tomatoes) and cherry or grape tomatoes. Romas are sweet and rich, with thick flesh and not a lot of seeds—and though they're excellent raw, they're even better cooked. Cherry or grape tomatoes are super-sweet, with dense, firm flesh and thin skin.
• Never store your fresh tomatoes in the fridge. Keep them somewhere dark and cool for optimum texture.

cook's note
Out of pasta except lasagna? Make pasta "rags" by breaking up lasagna noodles into smaller, bite-size pieces and cook until al dente.

shopsmart
Ricotta salata is aged ricotta—it's mild, crumbly, and slightly salty, like a mellower cousin of feta cheese (a perfect substitute).

spaghetti with meat sauce

makes 5 cups (enough for 1 pound of pasta or 4 to 6 servings) • prep time: 35 minutes

2 tablespoons extra-virgin
   olive oil
8 ounces ground beef (chuck is
   tastier and cheaper; sirloin
   is leaner)
1 medium onion
2 28-ounce cans whole peeled
   tomatoes
   Pinch sugar
   Freshly grated nutmeg
   (optional)
1½ teaspoons kosher salt, plus
   more for pasta-cooking water
   and to taste
   Freshly ground black pepper
1 pound spaghetti
1 sprig fresh basil leaves
½ cup freshly grated grana-style
   cheese, such as Parmesan

grating nutmeg

1. In a large soup pot or Dutch oven, heat olive oil over medium heat. Add the meat, breaking it up with a wooden spoon, and cook until it loses its rosy color, about 3 minutes. Meanwhile, chop the onion and add to the meat, stirring occasionally, until golden brown, about 5 minutes.

▶ know-how 99

2. Pour tomatoes and their juices into a large bowl and crush with your hands. Add the crushed tomatoes, sugar, nutmeg, if using, 1½ teaspoons salt, and some black pepper to the meat. Adjust the heat to maintain a simmer and cook the sauce, stirring occasionally, until it gets thick, about 25 minutes.

3. Meanwhile, bring a large pot of cold water to a boil over high heat and salt it generously. Drop the spaghetti into the boiling water and give it a stir. Cook, stirring occasionally, to make sure the noodles don't stick together.

4. Rinse and chop the basil leaves and stir into the sauce.

5. When the pasta is almost done (taste it—it should still be a little chewy), carefully lift it out of the water with tongs; let most of the water drip off and transfer the pasta to the sauce. Stir and turn the pasta with the tongs to coat evenly with sauce. Cook over medium-high heat until the pasta absorbs some of the sauce and is just tender, 1 to 2 minutes. If the pasta seems dry, add a splash of a little pasta water to keep it saucy. Remove pan from heat; stir in cheese. Divide among 4 warm serving bowls and serve.

canned tomato wisdom

Canned tomatoes are perfect for sauce. They're super-handy to have around because they last forever; they come already peeled (you don't always have to peel tomatoes, but peeled tomatoes are best for cooking); and, since they're canned at the peak of ripeness, you don't lose out on flavor. Here we generally call for canned whole tomatoes and have you crush them with your hands (or kitchen scissors), but diced work just as well for quick sauces.

shopsmart
Fresh whole nutmeg is sold in the spice aisle. It looks like a small, hard, brown grape. It does taste best freshly ground—it's got a warm, nutty richness that adds depth and flavor to sauces.

farfalle with tomato & roasted red pepper sauce
serves 4 • prep time: 25 minutes

1 teaspoon kosher salt, plus more for pasta-cooking water and to taste
3 large cloves garlic
⅓ cup drained oil-packed sun-dried tomatoes
½ cup jarred roasted red peppers
1 28-ounce can plum tomatoes
2 tablespoons extra-virgin olive oil
⅛ teaspoon crushed red pepper flakes
1 teaspoon sugar
   Freshly ground black pepper
2 handfuls fresh basil leaves
1 tablespoon balsamic vinegar
12 ounces farfalle pasta (bowties) (about ¾ of a box)
½ cup fresh ricotta cheese (optional)

1. Bring a large pot of cold water to a boil over high heat and salt it generously.

2. Meanwhile smash, peel, and chop the garlic. Coarsely chop the sun-dried tomatoes and roasted peppers. Pour the canned tomatoes and their juices into a large bowl and crush with your hands.

▶ know-how 99

3. Heat the olive oil in a large skillet over medium heat. Stir in the garlic, sun-dried tomatoes, roasted peppers, and red pepper flakes. Cook until the garlic is fragrant, about 1 minute. Add the crushed tomatoes, sugar, the 1 teaspoon salt, and some black pepper. Bring to a boil over high heat, then reduce to a simmer. Cook, uncovered, until thickened, about 10 minutes. Chop the basil. Remove the sauce from the heat; stir in the basil and balsamic; cover and set aside for about 10 minutes to let the flavors come together.

4. Drop the farfalle into the boiling water. Stir occasionally to make sure they don't stick together. When the pasta is al dente, drain in a colander, saving about ½ cup cooking water. Over medium heat stir and turn the pasta in the skillet with tongs to coat with sauce. If the pasta seems dry, splash in a little pasta water to keep it saucy. Season with salt and black pepper to taste. Divide among 4 warm serving bowls. Spoon a generous dollop of fresh ricotta on each serving, if desired.

ricotta wisdom
Ricotta, in Italian, means "recooked." It's made from whey left over from making mozzarella. It's a rich, sweet cheese textured like thick sour cream. It's got a short shelf life, so use it up quickly; drizzle it with honey for an easy dessert.

TIPS

shopsmart
There's lots of concentrated tomato flavor in sun-dried tomatoes, which makes them excellent for quick-cook sauces. Buy the jarred, packed-in-oil kind for the best possible taste.

quick marinara sauce
makes about 3 cups, enough to coat a pound of pasta • prep time: 20 minutes

¼ medium onion
3 cloves garlic
2 tablespoons extra-virgin
     olive oil
2 teaspoons kosher salt
1 28-ounce can whole, peeled
     tomatoes with juices
   Sprig fresh thyme
   Sprig fresh basil
   Freshly ground black pepper

1. Chop the onion and smash and peel garlic. Heat oil in a medium saucepan over medium-high heat. Add onion, garlic, and 1 teaspoon of the salt. Cook, stirring, until lightly browned, about 5 minutes. Use scissors to snip tomatoes into pieces in the can (or squeeze them through your hands to break them up). Add tomatoes with juices and herb sprigs to the pan and bring to a boil. Lower heat and simmer, covered, for 12 to 15 minutes.

know-how 99

2. Remove and discard the herb sprigs. Stir in the remaining salt and season to taste with black pepper. Serve immediately or store covered in the refrigerator for up to 3 days, or freeze for up to 2 months.

upgrades
To turn this into Creamy Vodka Sauce, add ½ cup heavy cream to the finished sauce and simmer for 3 to 5 minutes. Off the heat, stir in 2 to 3 tablespoons vodka and serve with penne or fusilli.

alcohol wisdom
Adding alcohol to food intensifies the flavors that are already there. Sometimes, like in the whiskey sauce on page 235, you want both the intensified flavor and the taste of alcohol; when you're making vodka sauce, you don't, so using flavorless vodka gets the job done. Since you're not cooking the sauce after adding vodka, the alcohol's still present and hasn't cooked off.

Clean as you go. Take a moment to straighten up before you start to assemble the lasagna. Put all the ingredients into separate bowls, then line the bowls up in the order you need them. Chefs call this "mise en place," but you can call it "being prepared."

lasagna serves 6 to 8 • prep time: 1 hour 30 minutes

white sauce
3 tablespoons unsalted butter
¼ cup all-purpose flour
4 cups milk
3 cloves garlic
1 teaspoon kosher salt
   Pinch cayenne pepper
   Pinch freshly grated nutmeg

lasagna
12 lasagna noodles
1 10-ounce box frozen spinach, thawed
2 tablespoons extra-virgin olive oil, plus more for greasing the baking dish
12 ounces sweet or hot Italian sausage (about 4 links)
½ teaspoon kosher salt, plus more for pasta cooking water

2 handfuls lightly packed fresh basil leaves (about 1 cup)
1¼ cups freshly grated grana-style cheese, such as Parmesan or pecorino Romano
3 cups Quick Marinara Sauce (page 121) or prepared tomato sauce, at room temperature
   Freshly ground black pepper

1. Preheat the oven to 350°F. Bring a large pot of cold water to a boil over high heat and salt it generously.

2. For the white sauce: Melt the butter in a medium skillet over medium heat. Stir in the flour with a wooden spoon and cook until the mixture darkens slightly in color, about 2 minutes. Whisk in the milk and bring to a boil. Smash and peel the garlic. Reduce the heat to maintain a gentle simmer and add the garlic. Cook, whisking occasionally, until thick (about the consistency of yogurt), about 20 minutes. Season with salt, cayenne, and nutmeg.

know-how 99

3. For the lasagna: Add the lasagna noodles to the boiling water and cook until al dente. Drain, but do not rinse, and lay each noodle out flat on a work surface.

4. Lightly grease a 9x13-inch baking dish with some olive oil. Use your hands to squeeze as much

water as you can from the spinach; set aside. Heat 2 tablespoons olive oil in a large skillet over medium heat. Cut the casing down the length of the sausages and remove the meat or squeeze the meat out of one end of the casing. Discard the casings. Crumble sausage and spinach into skillet and add the ½ teaspoon salt. Cook until sausage is no longer pink and spinach is tender and dry, about 5 minutes. Tear the basil leaves over the mixture and toss.

5. Cover the bottom of the prepared baking dish with 3 of the noodles. Top with ¼ cup grated cheese, ¾ cup tomato sauce, ½ cup white sauce, and ⅓ of the sausage mixture. Season with

some black pepper. Add another layer of 3 noodles. Repeat twice and dot the top layer of noodles with the remaining tomato sauce, white sauce, and grated cheese, making sure to dot some tomato sauce around the edges so that the noodles don't dry out. Bake, uncovered, until hot and bubbly, about 45 minutes. Let lasagna stand for 10 minutes before serving.

lasagna wisdom
Lasagna freezes and reheats beautifully. After baking and letting it rest, freeze it whole or in portions. Reheat in the microwave for lasagna anytime.

whisking in milk

checking consistency

outside-the-box pasta pie serves 4 to 6 • prep time: 35 to 40 minutes

1   teaspoon kosher salt, plus more
    for pasta-cooking water
8   ounces penne or penne rigate
½   cup milk
2   large eggs
1   tablespoon Dijon mustard

Dash Worcestershire sauce
Pinch freshly grated nutmeg
Freshly ground black pepper
2   slices bacon
½   medium onion
¼   cup drained oil-packed
    sun-dried tomatoes

1   tablespoon unsalted butter, plus
    more for greasing the pie dish
2   cups frozen broccoli florets,
    thawed
2   ounces cream cheese
2   cups shredded sharp
    cheddar cheese

1. Preheat the oven to 350°F. Bring a large pot of cold water to a boil over high heat and salt it generously. Add penne and boil, stirring occasionally, until al dente, about 6 to 8 minutes. Meanwhile, whisk milk, eggs, mustard, Worcestershire, nutmeg, and some black pepper in a large bowl. Drain the penne, let cool for a few minutes, then add to the bowl.

2. Slice the bacon crosswise into thin strips. Roughly chop the onion and sun-dried tomatoes. Melt the butter in a medium skillet over medium-high heat and cook the bacon until it begins to crisp, 3 to 4 minutes. Add the onion, sun-dried tomatoes, and broccoli to the skillet. Season with 1 teaspoon salt and some black pepper and cook until onion is tender, about 5 minutes. Toss the vegetable mixture with the pasta, cream

cheese, and 1½ cups of the cheddar until cream cheese melts.

▶ know-how 99

3. Grease a 9-inch pie dish with some butter and mound the pasta mixture in the dish. Scatter the remaining ½ cup cheddar over top. Bake on a baking sheet until pie is set and the top is golden brown and crisp, about 25 minutes. Let cool slightly before serving.

al dente noodle

TIPS

cook's note
If you have a pair of kitchen shears, use those to make quick work of snipping the bacon.

shopsmart
Penne rigate are lined with little ridges, giving them more of a grip on sauce.

couscous with carrots & raisins serves 6 • prep time: 15 minutes

3   medium carrots
1   lemon
2   tablespoons extra-virgin olive
     oil or unsalted butter
¼   teaspoon ground cinnamon
     Pinch ground ginger
3   cups water or chicken broth
⅔   cup golden raisins
1   teaspoon kosher salt
1½   cups regular or whole wheat
     couscous

1. Peel the carrots and slice into thin coins. Peel a long strip of zest from the lemon with a vegetable peeler.

▶ know-how 100, 104

2. Heat olive oil in a medium saucepan over medium heat. Toast cinnamon and ginger in oil until fragrant, about 1 minute. Add carrots, lemon zest, water, raisins, and salt and bring to a boil over high heat. Stir in couscous; remove from heat, cover, and set aside until the liquid is absorbed and the couscous is plump and tender, about 10 minutes. Fluff the couscous with a fork, discard the strip of lemon zest, and serve.

upgrades

• Add a handful of chopped fresh herbs, such as mint, cilantro, or parsley, when fluffing the couscous.
• Add other dried fruit, such as chopped apricots or figs, when stirring couscous into boiling water.

couscous wisdom

• Couscous, a staple food throughout the Middle East, is small grainlike pasta made from semolina flour. Most couscous that you buy in the U.S. has been precooked, so all you need to do is add boiling water to plump it up and it's ready to serve.
• It's great served with stews—or make it a meal by adding cooked vegetables. And a warm bowl of plain couscous with melted butter makes excellent comfort food.

cold sesame noodles serves 4 to 6 • prep time: 15 minutes

Kosher salt
8   ounces whole wheat spaghetti
1   tablespoon dark sesame oil
½   lime
¼   cup creamy natural peanut
    butter
2   tablespoons soy sauce
1   tablespoon light brown or
    white sugar
1½ teaspoons rice vinegar
¼   to ½ teaspoon crushed red
    pepper flakes
1   small Kirby cucumber
    (see page 102)
3   scallions
    Handful fresh cilantro leaves
½   cup mung bean sprouts

1. Bring a large pot of cold water to a boil and salt it generously. Add the spaghetti and cook, stirring occasionally, until al dente, about 8 minutes. Drain in a colander set in the sink, reserving about ¼ cup pasta-cooking water. Rinse noodles under cool running water. Toss noodles with the sesame oil in a serving bowl.

2. Squeeze the lime juice into another medium bowl. Whisk the peanut butter, soy sauce, sugar, vinegar, and red pepper flakes together, thinning the sauce slightly with some of the reserved pasta water (a tablespoon at a time). Pour over the noodles and toss to coat evenly with the sauce.
▶ know-how 104

3. Halve the cucumber lengthwise, then thinly slice. Thinly slice both the white and green parts of the scallions. Roughly chop the cilantro.
▶ know-how 102, 99, 103

4. Scatter the cucumber, scallions, bean sprouts, and cilantro over the noodles. Serve at room temperature.

shopsmart
TIPS
• Look for fresh mung bean sprouts in plastic tubs in the produce section. Don't bother with the canned ones if you can't find fresh.
• Dark sesame oil is made from roasted sesame seeds and tastes nutty and rich. It's more of a seasoning than a cooking oil, and it's packed with flavor, so a little goes a long way. Buy a small bottle, keep it in the fridge, and try to use it up within a few months. Give it a quick sniff before you use it; it should smell warm and toasty, not like damp cardboard.
• Whole wheat pasta is darker and a little denser than regular pasta; it's healthier too, and its nutty flavor goes really well with the sesame sauce. Brands differ; shop around to find the taste and texture that most appeals to you.

thai rice noodles serves 4 • prep time: 35 minutes

8 to 10 ounces medium-thick rice noodles (also called rice sticks or jantaboon)	3 tablespoons soy sauce	1 cup mung bean sprouts
3 tablespoons fish sauce	4 scallions	2 handfuls fresh mint or basil leaves (about 1 cup)
3 tablespoons sugar	1 jalapeño	½ cup cashews or peanuts
	3 cloves garlic	1 lime
	2 tablespoons peanut oil	

1. Put the rice noodles in a bowl with hot water to cover. Soak until tender and pliable, about 30 minutes.

2. While the noodles soak, prepare the rest of the ingredients. In a small bowl whisk together the fish sauce, sugar, and soy sauce; set aside. Trim scallions and thinly slice white and green parts. Halve the jalapeño lengthwise and remove the stem. For a milder dish, scrape out seeds with the tip of your knife; for more heat, leave the seeds in. Finely chop the jalapeño. Smash, peel, and roughly chop garlic.

▶ know-how 99

3. Drain the noodles and set aside. Heat a large skillet over high heat. Add the oil and, when hot, add the scallions, jalapeño, garlic, and bean sprouts. Cook, stirring, until the vegetables begin to brown and the garlic is fragrant, about 1 minute. Add the sauce mixture; gently swirl around the pan. Add the drained noodles and toss to coat them with the sauce. Remove the skillet from the heat and coarsely tear the mint into the skillet. Sprinkle in the nuts. Toss a few more times to incorporate the mint and nuts and mound into a large serving bowl. Cut the lime into wedges and serve with the noodles.

upgrades

• Toss in 1 to 2 cups shredded cooked chicken, extra-firm tofu cubes, thinly sliced cooked pork tenderloin, or 1 pound ready-to-eat shrimp.
• Add a cup or so of quick-cooking vegetables, like snow peas, or sliced bell pepper or onion, along with the scallions. If you want to add longer-cooking vegetables, like broccoli or green beans, steam them most of the way before adding them to the pan.
• Add some chopped ginger along with the garlic, ¼ cup canned coconut milk along with the sauce, or sprinkle on some chopped chiles before serving.

tearing basil

draining noodles

TIPS

shopsmart

Fish sauce is the Southeast Asian equivalent of Worcestershire sauce: It's pungent, salty, and adds a hit of complexity to dishes. Despite the name, it doesn't taste fishy—it's got a unique, unmistakably authentic flavor. Look for translucent, amber-color sauce in ethnic markets or the international aisle of your store. Keep it in a cool, dark cupboard for up to 2 years.

chicken, *etc.*

A cook's best friend and a totally blank slate—it works with a world of different flavors.

chicken wisdom

buy

- Chicken comes labeled as broiler-fryer, roaster, or stewing. These reflect size, not necessarily hard-and-fast rules for how to cook them. You can roast, fry, or stew any size of chicken, though huge roaster chickens can be a little hard to broil.
- The more taking-apart that's been done to a chicken, the more expensive it is per pound. That's why boneless, skinless chicken breasts cost more than the bone-in, skin-on kind. If you can't find skinless chicken, buy skin-on and just pull the skin off yourself.
- White or dark meat? White meat's leaner and cooks faster; dark meat is more flavorful and generally costs less. Dark's better for stewing; white's better for quick dinners. Cutlets (also called scaloppini) are thin cuts from the breast; they're good for pan-frying.
- Chicken can be free-range to natural to organic to none of the above. Regular supermarket chicken is reliable and inexpensive, but fresh organic chicken gives real meaning to "tastes like chicken." Kosher chickens are extra juicy and full of flavor.
- Think about 6 ounces of boneless meat per person or 8 ounces of bone-in. A 3-pound whole chicken should feed between 2 and 4 people, depending on what else you serve.
- We call for chicken breast halves in our recipes; the terminology changes depending on where you are. Technically, a "chicken breast" is the entire breast of the chicken, composed of two halves. One boneless breast half is about 4 to 6 ounces and about the size of your hand.

store

- Cook chicken within 2 days of buying, or freeze it.
- Keep raw chicken on the bottom shelf of the fridge, all the way in the back and away from other foods.
- Wrap individual servings well in plastic wrap to freeze and stick them in the bottom of the fridge to thaw the night before you plan on using them.
- If you need a speed-defrost, submerge the wrapped chicken in cold water for an hour or two; avoid countertop-defrosting.

prep & cook

- Don't wash chicken. Cooking it properly—to an internal temperature of 180°F in the thigh (see page 139 for just where to test it)—kills all the bacteria. Washing it just gets that bacteria all over the sink.
- Use a separate cutting board for raw chicken and wash your hands, knives, and everything else thoroughly (with hot water and soap!) after touching chicken. Good kitchen habits are paramount for poultry; check out page 13 for the basics of food safety.

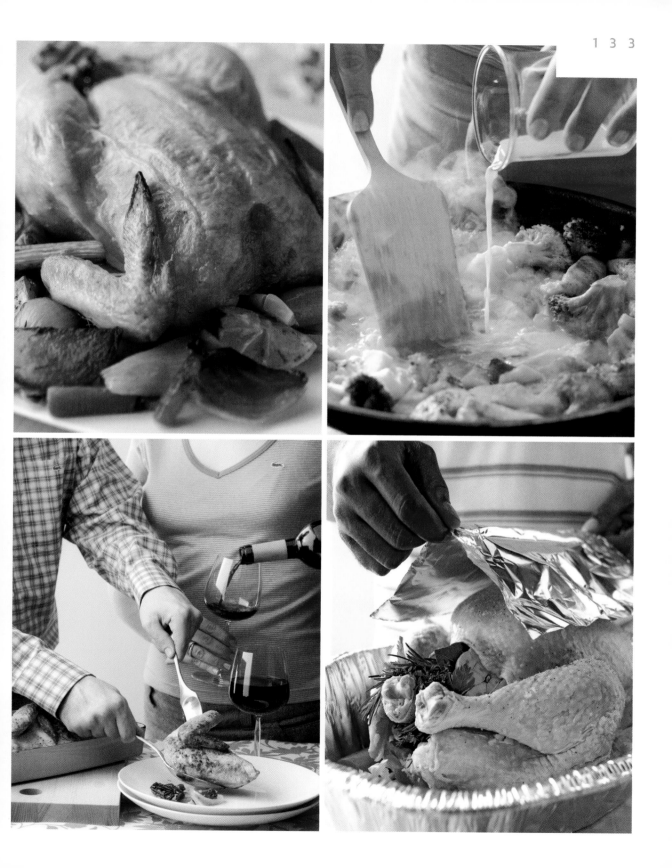

chicken with mustard pan sauce serves 4 • prep time: 20 minutes

4   boneless chicken breast halves,
     with skin (about 2 pounds)
     Kosher salt and freshly ground
     black pepper
2   tablespoons vegetable oil

½   cup white wine or dry white
     vermouth
1½ cups low-sodium chicken broth
     (about ¾ small can)

1   tablespoon all-purpose flour
2   tablespoons water
2   tablespoons whole-grain
     mustard
1   tablespoon unsalted butter
     (optional)

1. Preheat the oven to 350°F.

2. Heat a large skillet over medium-high heat. Pat chicken dry with paper towels and season all over with salt and black pepper. Add the oil to the hot pan and swirl to evenly coat. Lay the chicken pieces in the pan, skin side down, and cook without moving them until the skin crisps and browns, about 5 minutes. Flip and cook for another 3 minutes. Transfer chicken to a baking dish, skin side up, and bake until cooked through, about 10 minutes.

3. Pour the wine into the hot skillet. Use a wooden spoon to scrape up the browned bits in the bottom of the pan. Boil until almost all the wine evaporates and it gets a little syrupy, about 3 minutes. Add the broth and bring to a boil.

4. Mix the flour and water together to make thin paste (that's a "slurry"). Then whisk the slurry and mustard into the broth and boil until the sauce thickens,

1 to 2 minutes more. Remove pan from the heat. Swirl in the butter, if using, to give the sauce a little richness; season with salt and black pepper to taste. Add any collected juices from the chicken to the sauce. Put chicken on a plate, pour the sauce on top, and serve.

make it your own
· Add a sprig or 2 of chopped fresh herbs, like thyme, sage, or rosemary with the broth.
· Add 2 to 4 tablespoons heavy cream instead of the butter for a cream sauce; skip the slurry, then, and just boil until thick.
· You can cook pork chops the same way.

pan-sauce wisdom
A major reward of sautéing is a pan sauce—it's easy, tasty, fancy-looking, and impressive, with minimal cleanup and a lot of room for improvisation. Instead of white wine use red or substitute a smaller amount of lemon juice or wine vinegar.

the words
Deglaze: See those crusty brown bits in the bottom of the pan? Pour some liquid in and scrape those up with a spoon. That's deglazing.
Reduce: After deglazing, turn the heat up. See how the liquid boils and then gets thicker? That's reducing, also known as evaporating. You can reduce cream, wine, broth, or juice, but not milk.

Slurry: A mixture of flour (or cornstarch) and water used to thicken broth-based sauces.

don't panic
If the wine flames when you add it, it's fine. Step back and shake the pan until the flames die down. If the sauce is sticky and too thick, add a splash of water.

chicken with balsamic & garlic serves 4 • prep time: 20 minutes

10	cloves garlic	
	Flour, for dredging	
4	boneless, skinless chicken breast halves (about 2 pounds)	

Kosher salt and freshly ground black pepper
2   tablespoons vegetable oil
¼   cup balsamic vinegar

1¼ cups low-sodium chicken broth
1   tablespoon all-purpose flour
2   tablespoons water
1   to 2 tablespoons butter (optional)

1. Preheat the oven to 350°F. Smash and peel the garlic.

 know-how 99

2. Heat a large skillet over medium-high heat. Put the flour on a large plate. Pat the chicken dry with paper towels and season all over with salt and black pepper. Dredge (coat) the chicken in the flour and shake off any excess. Add the oil to the hot pan and swirl to evenly coat. Lay the chicken in the pan smooth side down. Scatter the garlic around the chicken. Cook the chicken, turning once, until golden, about 5 minutes per side. (Turn the garlic a few times so it cooks evenly.) Transfer chicken to a baking dish and bake until cooked through, about 10 minutes. Leave the garlic in the skillet.

3. Pour the vinegar into the hot skillet. Use a wooden spoon to scrape up the browned bits from the bottom of the pan. Boil until almost all the vinegar evaporates and it gets a little syrupy, about 1 minute. Add the chicken broth and bring to a boil.

4. Mix the flour and water together to make a thin paste (that's a "slurry"). Whisk the slurry into the broth and boil until the sauce thickens, about 1 minute more. Stir in butter, if using. Season the sauce with salt and black pepper. Add any collected juices from the chicken to the sauce. Put chicken on a plate, pour the sauce and garlic on top, and serve.

make it your own

If you've got some bacon fat left over (refrigerated) from breakfast, sauté the chicken in that—the salty baconyness is excellent with the vinegary sauce.

shopsmart

Balsamic vinegar is sweet, tart, and goes great with olive oil or flavorful greens. It's made by boiling down the juice of a certain kind of grape, fermenting it, then aging it in wooden casks. We like black balsamic, not white. There are also extra-aged traditional balsamics that are rich, full of flavor, and super-expensive—those are best saved for drizzling on roasted vegetables or fresh strawberries (strange, but wonderful).

chicken for one

This dish is infinitely rescalable. If it's just you, make one chicken breast and reduce the sauce ingredients by half.

TIPS

pan-frying (aka sautéing) wisdom

1. Heat the pan first. Let it get nice and hot before you add oil to it (2 minutes over medium low works as a general rule). If you're going to make a pan sauce, a heavy-bottomed regular pan is best—the crusty brown bits that form when you're sautéing make for tasty sauce—but nonstick works too.

2. Use a light touch with the oil—if the pan's hot enough, you won't need that much oil. Always give the oil a chance to warm up too.

3. Dry the food with a paper towel and season it generously with salt and black pepper just before it goes in the pan.

4. Put the nice side (the side you want face up when it's on the plate; if it's chicken, that means the skin side) down first to take advantage of the initial heat of the pan. Don't move it! Let it sit there until it's nice and golden; then it'll release from the pan on its own.

5. Put cuts too thick to cook through before the outside burns in a 350°F oven after browning on the stove. When done, transfer the food to a plate and keep it in a warm spot while you make the sauce in the pan.

① pan with drippings
  (+) liquid (wine, vinegar, cider, lemon juice)
② deglaze, reduce
③ (+) another liquid (broth, cream)
④ (+) slurry to thicken, if needed   = fabulous homemade sauce
⑤ (+) flavoring (mustard, herbs, spices, cheese)
⑥ (+) salt, pepper, a little butter (optional)

dredging

reducing

swirling in butter

roast chicken & vegetables serves 2 to 4 • prep time: 1 hour 30 minutes

3 tablespoons unsalted butter or
  extra-virgin olive oil
1 medium-large red or
  yellow onion
4 medium carrots
2 ribs celery

4 medium or 8 small red potatoes
4 to 8 cloves garlic
1 lemon
½ bunch fresh thyme
½ teaspoon kosher salt, plus more
  for seasoning

  Freshly ground black pepper
1 roasting chicken, about
  4 pounds
1 cup low-sodium chicken broth
  (½ small can)

1. Preheat the oven to 375°F. If using butter, melt it in a small saucepan or covered in the microwave. Halve and peel the onion; trim, but leave the root end intact; cut each half into 3 wedges. Peel carrots and halve lengthwise if very fat and cut into 2- to 3-inch wedges. Cut the celery into 2- to 3-inch pieces. Quarter the potatoes if large, halve if small. Smash and peel the garlic. Quarter the lemon.

▶ know-how 99, 100

2. Toss prepared vegetables, two lemon quarters, and 3 sprigs of thyme in a roasting pan with about a tablespoon of the butter and season with the ½ teaspoon salt and some black pepper. Season cavity of chicken with additional salt and black pepper. Tuck the rest of the thyme and remaining 2 lemon quarters into cavity of the chicken. Tie legs together with kitchen string if you have it (unwaxed dental floss works in a pinch). Set chicken, breast side up, on the bed of vegetables, brush or drizzle remaining butter over the skin, and season with salt and black pepper.

3. Roast the chicken for 1 hour. Give the vegetables a quick stir and then increase the oven temperature

to 425°F. Continue to cook until an instant-read thermometer inserted into the thickest part of the chicken thigh registers between 175°F to 180°F, and the skin is crisp and golden, about 15 minutes more.

4. Turn off oven. Let chicken rest out of the oven 5 minutes. Transfer vegetables to a platter; tip chicken so all its juices run back into the roasting pan. Transfer the chicken to a platter and surround with the vegetables. Return platter to the warm oven while you make the sauce (leave the door ajar if the oven still feels very hot).

5. Set the roasting pan on a burner over medium-high heat and stir with a wooden spoon to release the brown bits clinging to the pan. Whisk in broth and continue to stir. Bring to a boil and cook until slightly thicker, about 5 minutes. Transfer to a bowl or small pitcher.

6. Carve the chicken according to the method on page 153 and serve with roasted vegetables and sauce.

chicken wisdom

• Chicken's done when the internal temperature at the thigh reaches 180°F. It continues to cook even out of the oven, so if you take it out at 175°F, it'll get to 180°F while it rests.
• White meat cooks faster than dark, so if the breasts are done and the thighs are slightly pink, it's perfectly fine to put the legs back in the oven after carving. How you like your chicken is pretty personal; as long as it's over 180°F, it's fine.

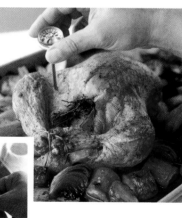

here's where to take the temp

tie legs together

chicken & broccoli stir-fry serves 4 • prep time: 30 minutes

1 bunch broccoli (about 1 pound)
2 cloves garlic
1 1-inch piece fresh ginger
1 pound chicken stir-fry strips
   (or whole boneless,
   skinless chicken breasts; see
   Cook's Note, below)
1 tablespoon soy sauce
1 tablespoon sugar
1 tablespoon plus 1 teaspoon
   cornstarch
1¼ teaspoons kosher salt, plus
   additional for seasoning
1 tablespoon dry sherry
1 tablespoon dark sesame oil
⅓ cup chicken broth or water
3 tablespoons vegetable oil
2 tablespoons water
   Freshly ground black pepper

for serving:
Cooked white rice (optional)

1. Cut broccoli tops into bite-size florets. Peel and thinly slice the broccoli stems, keeping stems and florets separate. Smash, peel, and chop garlic; peel and chop ginger.

▶ know-how 101, 99

2. Toss the chicken strips, half the garlic and ginger, the soy sauce, sugar, 1 teaspoon of the cornstarch, 1 teaspoon of the salt, the sherry, and sesame oil in a bowl. Marinate at room temperature for 15 minutes. Dissolve the remaining cornstarch in the broth or water.

3. Heat a large nonstick skillet over high heat. Add 1 tablespoon vegetable oil. When the oil is hot, add the broccoli stems and stir-fry for 1 minute. Add the florets, the remaining garlic and ginger, and 2 tablespoons water. Season with remaining salt and some black pepper. Stir-fry until the broccoli is bright green but still crisp, about 2 minutes. Transfer to a plate.

4. Get the skillet good and hot again and add remaining 2 tablespoons vegetable oil. Add the chicken and marinade. Stir-fry until the chicken begins to brown, about 4 minutes. Return the

broccoli to the pan and toss to heat through. Stir in the reserved cornstarch mixture and bring to a boil to thicken. Add a few tablespoons water or stock if the sauce seems too thick. Season with salt and black pepper to taste. Mound the stir-fry on a serving platter or divide among 4 plates; serve with rice, if desired.

stir-fry wisdom

Stir-frying works best on super-high heat. You don't need a wok to stir-fry; if you have one, use it, but if not, any wide-bottomed pan is fine. If you'd like to add other veggies, chop them up into bite-size pieces and add the slower-cooking ones (like green beans) earlier than the quick-cooking ones (like mushrooms).

cook's note

• The garlic and ginger can be chopped together in a mini chopper to save time.
• If using whole chicken breast, freeze for 20 to 30 minutes, then slice thinly across the grain (see page 163) to make strips. Thaw before using.

shopsmart

Dry sherry is a crisp, light wine that's nutty tasting and great for both stir fries and pan sauces. The way it's made means it'll keep for at least a month in the fridge. You don't have to buy an expensive bottle, but avoid cooking sherry.

chicken curry *serves 4 • prep time: 1 hour*

5	cloves garlic
1	medium red onion
1	2-inch piece fresh ginger
2	cups cold water
2	tablespoons vegetable oil
2	teaspoons Madras-style curry powder
½	teaspoon ground cumin
½	teaspoon ground cardamom (optional)
	Pinch cayenne pepper
1	tablespoon tomato paste
1	bay leaf
½	teaspoon kosher salt
3	pounds skinless, bone-in chicken thighs and drumsticks (about 5 each)
	Small handful fresh cilantro
2	tablespoons plain yogurt
	Freshly ground black pepper
½	lemon

Equipment: blender or food processor

for serving:
Cooked basmati rice (optional)
Mango chutney (optional)

1. Smash and peel the garlic. Trim the onion; quarter and peel it. Peel the ginger and put it, the garlic, and onion in a blender or food processor with ¼ cup of the water. Blend to a coarse puree.

▶ know-how 99

2. Heat the oil in a large skillet over medium-high heat. Add the onion mixture, curry powder, cumin, cardamom, if using, and cayenne. Cook, stirring, until the mixture begins to stick to the bottom of the pan, about 5 minutes. Stir in tomato paste and cook until brick red, about 1 minute. Add the remaining 1¾ cups water, the bay leaf, salt, and chicken. Bring to a boil, cover, and reduce heat to medium-low. Simmer until the chicken is tender, about 30 minutes.

3. Transfer the chicken to a bowl. Raise the heat to high and boil the curry uncovered, stirring occasionally, until it gets thick and saucy, about 10 minutes more. Chop the cilantro. Stir in yogurt. Reheat the chicken in the sauce without boiling it; finish with some black pepper, a squeeze of fresh lemon juice, and the cilantro. Serve with rice and chutney, if desired.

▶ know-how 103

upgrades
Add chunks of cooked potatoes or carrots to the curry to round out the meal.

whole cardamom

TIPS

shopsmart
• Cardamom, though on the pricey side, is great in both savory and sweet food, like our apple pie on page 237. It's smoky, pungent, and fundamental to Indian (and Scandinavian) cooking.
• Curry powder is an approximation of Indian spice blends. It usually contains turmeric, cayenne, coriander, ginger, cumin, fennel, and black pepper; Madras curry powder is a little spicier than regular curry powder. Toasting it in a dry skillet over low heat until fragrant brings out its flavor.

a side of history
We're calling this recipe chicken curry, but in India, where this dish originates, it'd just be called "chicken and gravy."

date-night chicken serves 2 to 4 • prep time: 1 hour 30 minutes

8	cloves garlic	1	bay leaf	2	to 3 tablespoons chicken broth or water
1	medium onion	2	teaspoons kosher salt, plus more for seasoning		Handful fresh parsley or cilantro leaves (optional)
¾	cup pitted dates		Freshly ground black pepper		
¾	cup pitted green olives	1	chicken, quartered (about 3 to 4 pounds)		
1	lemon				
3	tablespoons extra-virgin olive oil	1	teaspoon ground cumin		

for serving:
Couscous

1. Preheat oven to 400°F.

2. Smash and peel the garlic cloves and put into a shallow baking dish or casserole. Halve and thinly slice the onion. Quarter the dates and add them to the dish. Scatter the olives on top.

▶ know-how 99

3. Peel 6 long strips of zest from the lemon with a vegetable peeler, add to the dish, then juice lemon over the top. Toss everything with half of the olive oil, the bay leaf, the 2 teaspoons salt and some black pepper.

▶ know-how 104

4. Put the chicken quarters, skin side up, on top of the onion mixture, brush with the remaining olive oil, and season with the cumin, some salt, and some black pepper. Bake until the chicken is golden brown and the onion mixture is tender and juicy, about 1 hour and 15 minutes.

5. Transfer the chicken to a serving platter, discard the bay leaf and stir the broth or water into the onions, dates, and olives to glaze them. Spoon the goodies around and on the chicken. Rinse and chop the parsley, if using, and scatter over the top.

olive wisdom

To quickly pit olives or dates, press down on them with the flat side of a knife, then pull the pits out with your hands (or just buy the pitted kind).

TIPS

shopsmart
• Green olives are picked when unripe, which makes them firmer than black olives and better suited for cooking.
• Buy plump, soft dates (sometimes called Medjool dates) with intact skin—it's best to buy them in clear plastic tubs so you know what you're getting.

cook's note
If you want to get a head start, this recipe can be prepared through Step 2 and refrigerated overnight. This is the perfect dish for when people come over, as it's a one-pot meal where everything's made in advance. Just pop it in the oven before your guests arrive and you're free to relax with cocktails when they get there.

conversation starters

If you're going to go through all the effort of hosting a dinner, remember that a good dinner has as much to do with the people around the table as the food on it. Don't worry about seating boy-girl-boy-girl, but do think about how people get along and how to make them the most comfortable. For example, imagine a group of six:

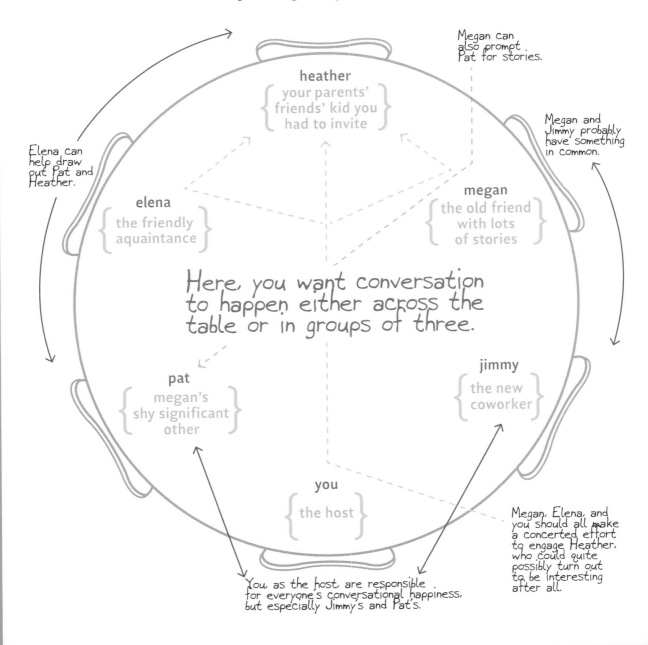

Megan can also prompt Pat for stories.

heather
{ your parents' friends' kid you had to invite }

Megan and Jimmy probably have something in common.

Elena can help draw out Pat and Heather.

elena
{ the friendly aquaintance }

megan
{ the old friend with lots of stories }

Here, you want conversation to happen either across the table or in groups of three.

pat
{ megan's shy significant other }

jimmy
{ the new coworker }

you
{ the host }

Megan, Elena, and you should all make a concerted effort to engage Heather, who could quite possibly turn out to be interesting after all.

You, as the host, are responsible for everyone's conversational happiness, but especially Jimmy's and Pat's.

people coming over?
Make your life easy and plan on having fun at your own party.

keep it simple with

- **make-ahead dishes or foods that taste good at room temp**
  If all you've got to do is dish up, you're free to hang out with your friends. Try the Date-Night Chicken (page 142), pot roast on page 166, or (for breakfast) Chocolate Chip-Banana Bread and some gorgeous fruit (pages 33 and 20, respectively). Make-ahead dishes like Gazpacho (page 70), Cold Sesame Noodles (page 127), or our Fusilli with Tomatoes & Basil (page 118) are all good cold; steak and aioli (page 163), Fried Chicken (page 147), or roasted veggies (pages 207-209) work at room temperature. Or serve a big salad, but dress it at the last minute to keep the greens crisp.
- **buffets and assemble-your-owns**
  Get everyone involved—do a taco bar with a few different fillings, or a salad bar, or even just an assortment of snacks. DIY dinner also gets a party going, as everyone has something to talk about (what they're eating, that they really hate cucumbers, whatever).
- **storeboughts and food finds**
  Shopping's part of cooking: Take pride in finding the best local sources for cheeses, meats, breads, cookies, and snacks. Or serve a home-cooked main dish alongside good bread or prebagged salad.
- **enlist recruits**
  Get your friends to help you out, either by bringing a dish or by lending a hand with cooking or washing dishes. People always end up in the kitchen anyway; make it work for you.

setting the scene

- **know your guests**
  Ask people what they don't eat before you plan. You don't want to have a pork-tastic feast all ready to go only to find out everyone's a vegetarian.
- **table (or floor) manners**
  You don't need to get too fancy, but having your table set before people come over is a nice touch. Real plates are great, but good-quality paper's fine too. And if you don't have a big enough table, spread out enough cushions so everyone can sit comfortably on the floor.
- **nosh & sip**
  Offer people a drink as soon as they get in and have a few snacks around for people to munch on before dinner.
- **encourage conversation**
  Make conversation easy: Keep low music in the background and the TV off (unless it's Food Network, in which case TV's allowed). Also, candles make every house look good but are by no means essential.
- **don't stress**
  Hanging out at home with friends is pretty great in and of itself, so you're already 99% there the minute you issue the invite.

In order: napkin (fold towards plate), fork, plate, glass (to the upper right), knife (blade towards plate), spoon. If you're a guest at a table with lots of silver, work from the outside in.

pb&j wings serves 4 to 6 • prep time: 25 minutes

1   1-inch piece fresh ginger
2   cloves garlic
1   tablespoon vegetable oil
1   12-ounce jar apricot jam
     (about 1 cup)
1   cup cider vinegar
2   tablespoons soy sauce
½   teaspoon Asian chile paste, such
     as sambal oelek
3   pounds whole chicken wings
     Kosher salt
     Peanut Sauce, homemade
     (below) or storebought,
     for dipping

This is perfect for grilled anything, or even with rice noodles.

peanut sauce

1   lime
½   cup natural peanut butter
⅓   to ½ cup chicken broth
1   tablespoon soy sauce
1   teaspoon Asian chile paste, such
     as sambal oelek
1   teaspoon sugar
     Kosher salt

Juice the lime into a medium bowl. Add peanut butter, ⅓ cup chicken broth, the soy sauce, chile paste, sugar, and salt to taste. Whisk until mixture resembles a smooth sauce. If it seems too thick, whisk in remaining broth to the desired consistency. Serve at room temperature.

1. Preheat oven to 450°F. Line a baking sheet with aluminum foil. Peel and roughly chop the ginger; smash and peel the garlic.

▶ know-how 99

2. Heat the oil in a small saucepan over medium-high heat, add the ginger and garlic, and stir-fry until brown, about 2 minutes. Add the jam, vinegar, soy sauce, and chile paste. Bring to a boil, reduce the heat, and simmer until the flavors come together, about 5 minutes.

3. Put wings in a large bowl. Pour jam mixture over the wings and toss to coat evenly. Pick the wings from the sauce, letting excess sauce drip back into the bowl; arrange on the prepared pan. Put remaining sauce in a saucepan.

4. Roast the wings, turning halfway through cooking, until firm, about 18 minutes for small wings and up to 25 minutes for bigger, meatier ones. Meanwhile, simmer the remaining jam sauce until thick, 15 to 20 minutes.

5. Turn on the broiler and broil the wings, turning halfway through, until they're richly colored and glossy, 3 to 5 minutes. Sprinkle broiled wings with salt to taste and dress with the jam sauce, tossing to coat. Transfer to a platter and serve immediately with the peanut sauce for dipping.

peanut butter wisdom

Natural peanut butter's more flavorful and lower in fat (and sugar) than the regular kind. Because it's unprocessed, the oil and the solids might separate; just stir them back together before using. It doesn't have any preservatives in it, so keep it in the fridge.

make it your own

Add ¼ cup chopped fresh herbs, such as mint, cilantro, or parsley, before serving.

whole vs. cut-up wings

TIPS **shopsmart**
Whole chicken wings are made up of three connected parts—the drummette, the flat, and the wingtip. If you can't find them, the separated kind are fine too—just remember, they cook faster than whole wings do.

fried chicken serves 4 • prep time: 45 minutes

1 broiler-fryer chicken, cut into 8 pieces (about 3 pounds)
  Kosher salt
2 cups all-purpose flour
1 tablespoon paprika
1½ teaspoons freshly ground black pepper
  Vegetable, soybean, or peanut oil, for deep-frying

1. Lay the chicken out on a cutting board. Pat dry. Adjust skin on the pieces so it covers the meat as evenly as possible. Trim any large excess pieces of skin or fat. Season the chicken with some salt.

2. Whisk the flour, paprika, and the black pepper in a large bowl. Bury the chicken pieces in the flour, in batches if necessary, to coat them completely. Lightly shake off any excess flour and return the coated chicken to the board so the flour "sets" while the oil heats up.

3. Heat about ¾ inch of oil in a large cast-iron skillet over medium heat until a deep-frying thermometer registers 350°F. Increase heat to high as you carefully lay the chicken, skin side down, in the fat, arranging the pieces so they fit easily in the pan. (Don't crowd the pan; cook chicken in batches if necessary or set up another pan if you have it.) Adjust heat to medium-high so chicken fries at an even crackle, but not too fast (the oil temperature should stay around 320°F to 325°F). Cover but leave a slight opening to release the steam. Cook until chicken is golden brown, about 10 minutes. Turn chicken with tongs

and fry, uncovered, until the other side is brown and crispy, about 8 minutes. Return chicken to the first side and cook until richly brown, 2 to 3 minutes more.

4. Remove the chicken from the oil and drain on a rack set over paper towels or simply on paper towels. Season with salt to taste and serve hot or at room temperature.

make it your own
Add other spices to the flour, such as 1 tablespoon curry, chili powder, Italian seasoning, or Chinese five-spice powder.

frying wisdom
When dealing with hot oil of any sort, be careful—never overfill the pan, avoid splashes, make sure everything you're frying is dry, and never put water on a grease fire. Use baking soda or salt, or smother the flame with a lid. Don't pour leftover oil down the sink; let it cool completely, pour it into a sealable container, and throw the container in the trash.

cook's note
There's nothing better than a deep cast-iron pan for frying, as it distributes heat perfectly. If you don't have a cast-iron pan, use a deep, heavy-bottomed skillet—nonstick coatings don't stand up well to that level of heat.

lemon-herb-marinated broiled chicken
serves 4 • prep time: 45 minutes

2 lemons
2 cloves garlic
  Small bunch mixed fresh herbs,
    such as flat-leaf parsley, sage,
    oregano, thyme, and rosemary
½ cup extra-virgin olive oil, plus
    additional for brushing
2 teaspoons kosher salt, plus
    more for seasoning
  Pinch crushed red pepper flakes
  Freshly ground black pepper
1 3- to 4-pound chicken, cut into
    8 pieces

1. Juice 1½ lemons into a dish large enough to hold the chicken. Cut the remaining half into wedges for garnish, if desired. Smash and peel the garlic. Strip the herbs from the stems and roughly chop; you should have about ½ cup chopped herbs. Whisk the olive oil, garlic, herbs, the 2 teaspoons salt, the crushed red pepper flakes, and some black pepper into the lemon juice. (Or just put the marinade together in a large resealable plastic bag and add the chicken pieces.) Trim away any excess fat from the chicken pieces before adding the chicken to the marinade, turning to coat evenly. Marinate at room temperature for 1 hour, turning once, or cover and refrigerate up to 12 hours.

▶ know-how 104, 99, 103

2. Position a rack 6 to 8 inches from the broiler and, if you have the option, turn the broiler to medium-low. Line a broiler pan with foil and set insert on top.

3. Remove the chicken from the marinade and season with some salt and black pepper. Arrange the chicken pieces, skin side down, on broiler pan with the largest pieces in the center so they'll be under the hottest part of the broiler. Broil until the chicken loses its raw color, about 10 minutes. Turn chicken skin side up, and continue to cook until the skin is crispy and golden brown and an instant-read thermometer inserted in the thickest part of each piece registers 170°F, 15 to 20 minutes more. Transfer to a large platter.

broiler pan wisdom
A broiler pan, which usually comes with your oven, is great for foods like chicken and steak; the fat drips down through the vents and doesn't flare up. Line the bottom pan with foil for easy cleanup.

juicing wisdom
Microwave lemons (or any citrus) for 5 seconds on low heat to make them easier to juice.

See page 167 for more on marinating.

shopsmart
TIPS Mixed fresh herbs (also sometimes called poultry herbs) are a blend of parsley, sage, oregano, thyme, and rosemary. If you can't find a mix, make your own: Use more leafy herbs (like parsley and sage) than woody ones (thyme, oregano, and rosemary), because a little of the woody ones goes a long way.

tuscan chicken stew

serves 4 • prep time: 1 hour

1 onion
4 cloves garlic
1 15-ounce can cannellini
  or Great Northern beans
8 bone-in skinless chicken thighs
  (about 3 pounds)
  Kosher salt and freshly ground
  black pepper
3 tablespoons extra-virgin
  olive oil
  Pinch crushed red pepper flakes
1 large sprig rosemary or
  1 teaspoon dried Italian
  seasoning
1 tablespoon tomato paste
½ cup dry red wine
1 14-ounce can chopped tomatoes
¾ cup chicken broth (about
  ½ small can)
1 small head escarole or 4 cups
  baby spinach leaves (about
  8 ounces)
½ cup freshly grated pecorino or
  Parmesan cheese (about
  1 ounce)

1. Chop the onion; smash and peel the garlic. Rinse and drain the beans in a colander or strainer.
▶ know-how 99

2. Heat a Dutch oven over medium-high heat. Pat chicken dry with paper towels and season all over with salt and black pepper. Add oil to the Dutch oven. When the oil is hot, add chicken, skinned (rounded) sides down, and brown, in batches if necessary, about 4 minutes per side. Transfer to a platter.

3. Reduce the heat to medium, add the onion, garlic, red pepper flakes, and herbs; cook, stirring until onions are slightly soft, about 5 minutes. Stir in the tomato paste and cook until brick red, about 1 minute. Add the wine and use a wooden spoon to scrape up any brown bits that cling to the pan. Bring to a boil and cook until syrupy, about 1 minute. Add the beans, tomatoes, and chicken broth, and bring to a boil. Nestle the chicken pieces in the stew, adding any collected juices to the pan. Simmer the stew, uncovered, until the chicken is cooked through, about 20 minutes.

4. Trim the escarole and tear the leaves into bite-size pieces. (If you're using baby spinach, there's no need to do this). Wash the escarole or spinach and drain. Add greens to the stew, cooking only until wilted, about 4 minutes. Stir in the cheese and season with salt and black pepper to taste. Serve in shallow bowls.

TIPS

shopsmart
Escarole's great. It's mildly flavored, much easier to clean than spinach (see cleaning instructions on page 78), has a melty-tender texture when it's cooked, and is packed full of vitamins A and C. If you can't find it, use other greens (like spinach, Swiss chard, or kale).

a side of history
Beans are a huge part of Tuscan cuisine—dating to at least the 17th century—to the extent that the rest of Italy calls Tuscans "bean-eaters."

roast turkey with gravy serves 8 • prep time: 3 hours 15 minutes

1 12- to 14-pound turkey
   Kosher salt and freshly ground
   black pepper
2 medium onions
1 head garlic
   Several sprigs of fresh herbs,
   like thyme, parsley, rosemary,
   or sage

2 bay leaves
2 to 4 medium carrots
2 to 4 celery ribs
8 tablespoons unsalted butter
8 cups chicken broth (about
   4 small cans or 2 quart boxes)

½ cup all-purpose flour
   Dash Worcestershire sauce

*Equipment: large roasting pan, pastry
brush or bulb baster, instant-read
thermometer*

1. Adjust an oven rack to the lowest position and remove the other racks. Preheat oven to 325°F.

Remove neck and giblets from the turkey. Discard the liver (it's the softest piece). Set the others aside. Dry the turkey inside and out with paper towels. Season the breast cavity with salt and black pepper. Slice the onions and halve the garlic head crosswise. Stuff all the garlic and half of the onions inside the turkey along with some of the herbs and 1 bay leaf. Halve the carrots and celery lengthwise; put them in the center of roasting pan and set the turkey, breast side up, on top of the vegetables.

▶ know-how 99

2. Melt butter in a medium saucepan and brush half of it all over the bird. Season skin with salt and black pepper. Tent turkey with aluminum foil and roast 2 hours. Set aside about 3 tablespoons of the butter for basting the bird.

3. Cook the rest of the onions, neck, and giblets in the remaining butter in a large saucepan over medium-low heat, stirring occasionally until browned, about 15 minutes. Add the broth and remaining herbs and bay leaf; cover and simmer while the turkey roasts, about 2 hours. Discard the giblets, if desired, or reserve for giblet gravy.

4. After 2 hours remove foil from turkey and use a pastry brush or bulb baster to baste turkey with reserved butter and some pan drippings. Increase oven temperature to 425°F and continue roasting until an instant-read thermometer inserted in the thigh (see page 139) registers between 170°F and 180°F, about 1 hour more. Transfer turkey to a cutting board. Discard or serve vegetables.

5. For the gravy: Pour all the turkey pan drippings into a liquid measuring cup. Spoon off ½ cup of the fat from the top of the drippings and transfer to a saucepan. (See Gravy Wisdom,

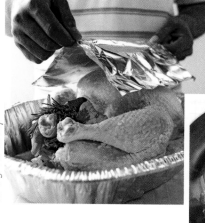

tenting the turkey

giblets & neck

degreasing

below right.) Heat the ½ cup fat over medium heat, scatter the flour evenly on top, and cook, stirring constantly, with a wooden spoon until the flour browns slightly and smells toasty, about 4 minutes. Switch to a whisk. Gradually and carefully ladle the hot broth into the flour mixture while whisking constantly. Bring the gravy to a boil; adjust the heat so it simmers gently. Skim and discard any excess fat from the remaining drippings, and add the pan juices to the gravy. Continue to simmer, whisking occasionally, until the gravy is thickened, about

10 minutes. Season with the Worcestershire and to taste with salt and black pepper.

6. Remove and discard onion, garlic, herbs, and bay leaf from the turkey cavity. Pour any juices that have accumulated into the gravy. Carve the turkey according to the method on the opposite page. Serve with vegetables if desired.

gravy wisdom

• If the pan drippings are really fatty, separate the fat out by pouring it into a liquid measuring cup and using a spoon to skim off the fat from the top. Stick it in the freezer to make the fat rise up faster. Or, if you have a degreasing cup (see photo below), use that. We love degreasing cups because they take the work out of separating fat; they have a low-on-the-cup spout that helps pour out the drippings and leave the fat behind.

• Once the broth is super hot, add it slowly, whisking constantly so there aren't any lumps. A whisk is essential for smooth gravy, but if you get lumps anyway, strain the gravy through a fine-mesh strainer (or a colander).

• Giblets make the tastiest gravy —yeah, turkey innards seem a little weird, but they really do add a lot of good flavor.

degreasing cup

TIPS

shopsmart
• Buying a fresh turkey will save you time, but if that's not possible, then go frozen and thaw it in the fridge for about 24 hours for every 5 pounds. Think about a pound per person for ample leftovers.

• The pop-up timers that come with turkey can be unreliable; invest in an instant-read thermometer and use that to determine the doneness. Stick it into the thickest part of the thigh (see the photo on page 139); it should register about 175°F.

how to carve a turkey

① Place turkey right side up on board. Slice skin near thigh to separate leg from body. As a general rule, angle knife toward bone when carving. Using a fork, pull leg downward and away from body until joint pops out. Cut through joint and along the body to separate leg.

② With leg skin side down, cut through joint to separate thigh from drumstick. It should be easy; if you feel resistance, wiggle the knife until you find the right spot.

③ Slice a small oval of skin (with breast meat attached) down towards the wing joint. Cut through wing joint (again, this should be easy) and remove the wing.

④ Starting at the top of the breast, make a long cut along one side of the center bone. Continue to cut along the bone, following the curve of the body, to free one side of the breast. Use a fork to gently pull meat away from body while you cut.

⑥ Hold drumstick upright and slice the meat away into 3 pieces (optional). Repeat whole process for the other side.

⑤ Cut breast into slices.

apple-cranberry dressing serves 8 to 10 • prep time: 1 hour 20 minutes

6   tablespoons unsalted butter, plus more for the pan
1   pound sliced country white sandwich bread
1   large cooking apple, such as Gravenstein or Golden Delicious
1   medium onion
2   celery ribs with leaves
½   cup dried apricots
     Handful fresh flat-leaf parsley leaves
2   to 3 sprigs fresh thyme
¼   cup dried cranberries
½   teaspoon kosher salt
     Pinch fennel seeds (optional)
3   cups chicken broth (about 1½ small cans)
1   large egg
2   tablespoons turkey or chicken pan drippings, or melted butter

1. Preheat oven to 325°F. Butter a shallow 3-quart casserole.

2. Cut or tear bread into bite-size pieces. Lay bread pieces in a single layer on 1 or 2 baking sheets. Bake until slightly dry and crisp, 15 to 20 minutes. Cool.

3. Peel, core, and coarsely chop the apple. Coarsely chop the onion, celery, and apricots. Chop parsley. Strip the leaves off the thyme.

▶ know-how 99, 100, 103

4. Melt the 6 tablespoons butter in a large skillet over medium-high heat. Add the apple, onion, celery, apricots, thyme, cranberries, salt, and fennel seeds, if using; cook until soft, about 5 minutes. Add the broth and parsley and bring to a boil. Remove from the heat.

5. Beat the egg in a large bowl. Add the toasted bread and the onion and fruit mixture; toss until evenly moistened. Loosely pack the dressing in the prepared pan. Bake, uncovered, until the top is crusty, about 40 minutes. Drizzle the pan drippings or melted butter over the top. Cook until the top is crisp and golden, about 20 minutes more.

upgrade
Cook 1 pound of crumbled bulk pork sausage until brown and crispy in the skillet. Remove to a plate and cook vegetables and fruit in the residual fat. Stir sausage into stuffing just before baking.

cook's note
TIPS Dressing's best when cooked outside a turkey (which is why we're not calling it stuffing); inside the bird, it lengthens the cooking time. It's easier on you to just stick it in the oven during the last hour of turkey-cooking.

italian turkey meatballs

serves 4 to 6 • prep time: 35 minutes, plus 1 hour inactive

2 cloves garlic
Large handful fresh flat-leaf parsley leaves
1/2 medium onion
1 1/2 pounds ground turkey
1/2 cup grated Parmesan, plus additional for serving
1/3 cup dried bread crumbs
2 teaspoons kosher salt
1 large egg, beaten
2 tablespoons milk
2 dashes Worcestershire sauce (about 1/2 teaspoon)
Freshly ground black pepper
1/4 cup extra-virgin olive oil
2 to 3 cups Quick Marinara Sauce (page 121) or storebought tomato sauce
1 pound hot cooked spaghetti or linguine, for serving (optional)

1. Smash, peel, and chop garlic. Chop the parsley (you should have about 1/4 cup). Peel and dice the onion (or grate on a box grater); you should have about 1/4 cup. Mix the turkey, onion, parsley, garlic, Parmesan, bread crumbs, salt, egg, milk, Worcestershire, and black pepper in a large bowl. Mix until just combined; don't overmix.

▶ know-how 99, 103

2. Using your hands, gently form mixture into 18 meatballs (slightly larger than golf balls). Put them on a plate; cover and refrigerate at least an hour or up to 24 hours.

3. Heat half the oil in a large nonstick skillet over medium-high heat. Add half the meatballs and cook, turning occasionally, until well browned on all sides, about 6 minutes. Transfer the meatballs to a plate and repeat with the remaining olive oil and meatballs.

4. Drain off the oil and wipe out the skillet. Return the meatballs to the skillet and pour in the tomato sauce. Bring to a boil, lower the heat, cover, and simmer until the meatballs are cooked through, about 15 minutes. Serve the meatballs with the sauce or toss with hot pasta and freshly grated Parmesan, if desired. The meatballs can be stored, covered, in the refrigerator for 3 days, or frozen for up to 6 weeks.

meatball wisdom

• Be gentle when you're forming meatballs—too firm a hand makes them dense and tough.
• These can be frozen cooked (in sauce) or raw; freeze raw meatballs on a cookie sheet, then transfer them to resealable plastic bags. Cooked-in-sauce meatballs can go into plastic containers.

flavor wisdom

Worcestershire sauce brings out the flavor in a dish. The reason why has to do with a concept called "umami." It's a way of describing "deliciousness" or "robustness" in Japanese. Use a dash of Worcestershire in soups, on burgers and steaks, or in Bloody Marys to make the flavor pop. (A sprinkling of Parmesan cheese has a similar effect.)

cook's note
TIPS We're using turkey here because it's lower in saturated fat than the more-traditional combination of beef, veal, and pork.

beef, pork & a little lamb

Master the basics, then play around: Change seasonings, tastes, and flavors to make it your own.

meat wisdom

Depending on the cut of meat and how you cook it, you end up with anything from a sink-your-teeth-in steak to a meltingly tender stew. Techniques you'll need to know:

broil
- Broiling—cooking with high heat from above—is one of the easiest ways to cook thin, lean cuts of meat, fish, and poultry. If you preheat the broiler pan (and the item is thin enough), you won't even have to flip the food.
- Broilers differ; some are hotter than others. Preheating is key. Put bigger pieces in the center, where it's hottest.

pan-fry
Pan-frying is sautéing—it's quick cooking in a skillet over direct high heat. It works best with thin cuts of meat like chops, steaks, and cutlets so the inside cooks before the outside has a chance to scorch.

roast & rest
- Roasting is cooking in the oven. (It's really the same as baking.) It's best-suited for large cuts of meat. High-heat roasting gets you quick and crisp results; low-heat roasting gets you soft and tender results.
- Always let cooked meat rest for a few minutes before serving or carving. This lets the juices stay in the meat, not on the cutting board.

sear & roast
- Some cuts—like lean loins, big steaks, or thick chops—can't be completely skillet-cooked; the outside scorches before the inside's done. They can be oven-roasted, but they'll finish cooking before the outside browns. Searing meat (that is, quickly pan-frying over high heat) before finishing in the oven gets you a rich brown crust along with a perfectly cooked interior.

braise
- Braising is low-temperature cooking in gently simmering liquid that comes halfway up the sides of the food. Braising makes the toughest (and cheapest) cuts tender and gives you a great sauce. It's also almost impossible to overcook braised meat. It does take time, but you end up with amazing results for very little effort.

tacos picadillo serves 4 to 6 (12 tacos) • prep time: 30 minutes

1   medium onion
2   cloves garlic
1   jalapeño
2   tablespoons extra-virgin
       olive oil
1½   tablespoons chili powder
1   teaspoon ground cumin
2   teaspoons kosher salt, plus
       more for seasoning
1   15.5-ounce can chopped
       tomatoes
12   ounces lean ground sirloin
       Handful fresh cilantro leaves
       Freshly ground black pepper
¼   head romaine or iceberg lettuce
1½   cups shredded cheddar cheese
12   prepared taco shells, or corn
       tortillas, preferably white

for serving:
Lime wedges

1. Peel and chop the onion
and garlic. Halve the jalapeño
lengthwise and remove the stem
(for less heat, scrape out the seeds;
for maximum heat, leave the seeds
in); chop the jalapeño.
▶ know-how 99

2. Heat a medium skillet
over medium heat and add the
olive oil. Add the onion, garlic,
jalapeño, chili powder, cumin, and
2 teaspoons salt and cook, stirring
occasionally, until tender, about
10 minutes. Increase the heat to
medium-high, add the tomatoes,
and boil until slightly thick, about
2 minutes. Stir in the sirloin and
adjust the heat so the mixture
simmers. Cook, breaking meat up
with a wooden spoon, until it loses
its raw color and the mixture is
thick, about 15 minutes. Roughly
chop and add the cilantro. Season
with salt and black pepper to taste.

3. Thinly slice the lettuce and put
in a serving bowl. Put the cheese
and meat in serving bowls and the
taco shells on a platter. If making
soft tacos, heat the tortillas (see
page 19). Serve and let guests build
their own tacos.

to make taco shells

Pour about 1½ inches of oil in a
small skillet. Heat over medium to
medium-high until the edge of a
tortilla sizzles briskly when dipped
in the oil. Holding one edge of a
tortilla with tongs, lay the other
half in the oil, keeping it flat with a
spatula. Cook until crisp, 1 minute.
Flip the tortilla over and repeat
with the other half, holding the
first side of the tortilla at an angle
to make an open shell; cook for 1 to
2 minutes more. Transfer to a plate
lined with paper towels.

make it your own

Traditional additions to picadillo
include olives, capers, potatoes,
and raisins—or mix it up with
chopped tomatoes, sliced avocado,
sliced canned jalapeños, or
shredded cabbage or radish.

TIPS

cook's note

There are few things better than a soft taco (the
classic way to serve tacos in Mexico). If you're into
the hard tacos, either fry the tortillas according to the
instructions above or buy hard taco shells and warm
them up in a low (200°F) oven for a few minutes before
serving dinner. See note on kinds of tortillas, page 41.

a side of history

"Picadillo" can probably be best translated as "hash."
It's thought to come from the Spanish "picar," which
means to chop up. There are versions of it all over the
Spanish-speaking world, but it's especially popular
in Cuba, where it's made with olives and raisins and
served over rice.

quick beef chili
serves 4 • prep time: 30 minutes

1	medium yellow onion
5	cloves garlic
1	chipotle chile en adobo, with 1 tablespoon of sauce
3	tablespoons extra-virgin olive oil
1	tablespoon kosher salt
2	teaspoons chili powder
1	teaspoon dried oregano
1	tablespoon tomato paste
1	pound ground beef chuck
1	cup Mexican lager-style beer (about ¾ of a bottle or can)
1	15-ounce can kidney beans
1	14½-ounce can whole peeled tomatoes, with their juices
1	cup chicken broth (about ½ small can)

for serving:
Grated Monterey Jack cheese or other Mexican cheeses (see page 184), sour cream, tortilla chips, cilantro sprigs and/or sliced scallions, for garnish (optional)

1. Peel and chop the onion and garlic. Finely chop the chipotle. Heat the olive oil in a large, heavy skillet over medium-high heat. Add the onion, garlic, salt, chili powder, and oregano and cook, stirring, until fragrant, about 3 minutes. Stir in the tomato paste and the chipotle chile and its sauce; cook 1 minute more. Add the beef, breaking it up with a wooden spoon, and cook until the meat loses its raw color, about 3 minutes. Add the beer and simmer until reduced by about half, about 5 minutes.

▶ know-how 99

2. Rinse and drain the beans in a colander. Add the tomatoes to the chili by crushing them through your fingers into the skillet and add the juices from the can. Add the broth and beans and bring to a boil. Cook, uncovered, stirring occasionally, until thickened, 8 to 10 minutes.

3. Ladle the chili into bowls and serve with the garnishes of your choice.

chipotle chile en adobo, chipotle hot sauce & dried chipotle

 TIPS

cook's note
A skillet's larger surface area reduces sauces faster than simmering them in a saucepan.

shopsmart
Chipotles are smoked jalapeño chiles. You'll usually see them canned en adobo (a vinegary sauce made from pureed chiles) in the Latin section of your store, near the salsas and canned beans. They're also sold dried or pureed with vinegar in hot sauce form.

a side of history
Chili's the kind of food that everyone's got an opinion on. There are all kinds of regional chili traditions, from Cincinnati's cinnamon-and-noodles to Texan cubed-meat-and-spices (with nothing else)—and there are countless books on the subject. If you're looking to become a chilihead (which is what the International Chili Society calls its members), check out our website (foodnetwork.com) for several hundred recipes.

cheesy meatloaf serves 4 to 6 • prep time: 1 hour 20 minutes

2	slices bacon
1	medium onion
3	cloves garlic
	Large handful fresh flat-leaf parsley leaves
1	large egg
1	tablespoon Dijon mustard
1	tablespoon Worcestershire sauce
1	teaspoon kosher salt
½	teaspoon freshly ground black pepper
2	pounds ground beef chuck
8	ounces shredded sharp Cheddar cheese (about 2 heaping cups)
¼	cup ketchup

1. Preheat oven to 400°F. Line a rimmed baking sheet or the bottom half of a broiler pan with foil.

2. Cook bacon in a medium nonstick skillet over medium-low heat until crispy, about 10 minutes. Meanwhile, chop onion and smash, peel, and chop garlic. Transfer the bacon to a plate lined with paper towels, leaving the bacon fat in the skillet. Add the onion and garlic and cook until softened, 5 to 8 minutes. Cool.

▶ know-how 99

3. Chop the parsley. Whisk the egg, mustard, Worcestershire, salt, and black pepper in a large bowl. Add ground beef, cheese, parsley, and the cooled onion mixture. Crumble in the bacon. Mix with a fork or your hands until evenly blended, but don't overmix.

▶ know-how 103

4. Dampen hands with water and pat the meatloaf mixture into a loaf shape on the prepared baking sheet. Bake for about 45 minutes, then brush the ketchup over the top of the meatloaf. Continue cooking until an instant-read thermometer inserted into the center of meatloaf registers 155°F, about another 15 minutes. Let the meatloaf rest for at least 10 minutes before slicing and serving.

make it your own

• Use a blend of 1 pound ground chuck, 8 ounces ground pork, and 8 ounces ground veal. This is sometimes labeled "meatloaf mix" in the butcher case.
• Add chili powder and a shot of hot sauce in with the ketchup or meat mixture.
• For a firmer loaf add ½ cup breadcrumbs or raw quick-cooking oatmeal.

TIPS **cook's note**
One of the best things about leftover meatloaf is the potential for meatloaf sandwiches; check out our sandwich chapter for inspiration.

If you're improvising meatloaf, you'll still want to season to taste. Fry up a small patty of the meat mixture so you know what the final product will taste like and adjust the seasoning accordingly.

flank steak with garlic mayonnaise (aioli)
serves 4 • prep time: 30 minutes

flank steak

- 2 tablespoons extra-virgin olive oil
- 1 tablespoon Dijon mustard
- ½ teaspoon Worcestershire sauce
- 2½ teaspoons freshly ground black pepper or pepper blend
- 1½ teaspoons kosher salt
- 1 flank steak, about 2 pounds

garlic mayonnaise (aioli)

- 1 large clove garlic
- ¼ teaspoon kosher salt
- 3 tablespoons mayonnaise
- ⅓ cup extra-virgin olive oil
- ½ lemon

1. For the flank steak: Line a broiler pan with foil and set insert on top. Position a rack so it's 5 to 6 inches from the broiler unit. Set prepared pan on the rack. The surface of the pan should be about 3 to 4 inches from the heat source. Heat pan for 10 minutes. Meanwhile, whisk together the oil, mustard, Worcestershire, black pepper, and salt in a small bowl. Rub onto both sides of the steak.

2. Carefully pull the preheated pan from the broiler. Set the steak in the center of the rack (it should sizzle when it hits the pan). Return pan to the broiler. Cook until the steak browns and feels somewhat firm but gives gently when pressed, 8 to 10 minutes for medium-rare. An instant-read thermometer inserted crosswise into the thickest part of the steak should read about 125°F. (If your broiler pan was preheated properly you won't have to turn the meat.) Remove meat

from the broiler and let it rest on a cutting board for 5 to 10 minutes while you make the aioli.

3. For the aioli: Smash the garlic clove, peel, sprinkle with the salt, and, with the flat side of a large knife, mash and smear the mixture to a paste. Set aside. Put the mayonnaise in a small bowl. Gradually whisk in the oil, starting with a few drops and then adding the rest in a steady stream, to make a smooth, slightly thick dressing. Whisk in the garlic paste. Squeeze in about 1 teaspoon lemon juice to thin it out a bit.

▶ know-how 99, 104

4. Thinly slice the meat against the grain and arrange on a platter. Serve warm or at room temperature with the aioli.

make it your own
Whisk 1 teaspoon tomato paste into the mayo mix or add hot sauce or minced herbs. Or substitute freshly squeezed orange or lime juice for the lemon.

TIPS

cook's note
Cuts like flank steak have long, chewy muscle fibers that need to be broken up for the best possible texture. When we say cut across the grain, look at the direction the muscle fibers are running, then slice across them.

a side of history
Aioli (aka garlic mayo) is a popular condiment throughout the Mediterranean. It's a great dipping sauce for fries, boiled or steamed vegetables, or crusty bread—and it's a classic with steak.

pan-seared t-bone steak with red wine sauce
serves 2 • prep time: 25 minutes

1	1½-pound T-bone steak (see page 169)
2	shallots

2	to 4 tablespoons unsalted butter
	Kosher salt and freshly ground black pepper

1	tablespoon vegetable oil
¾	cup dry red wine
¼	cup chicken broth

1. About ½ hour before you begin cooking, remove steak from refrigerator. Preheat the oven to 450°F. Trim, peel, and thinly slice the shallots. Cut the butter into small cubes and return to the refrigerator.

2. Heat a large, heavy-bottomed skillet over high heat. Pat the steak dry and season generously with salt and black pepper. Add the oil to the hot skillet. When it just begins to smoke, add the steak. Reduce heat slightly and cook until steak browns on one side, about 4 minutes. Turn and cook the other side for another 2 minutes, then transfer the steak to a baking dish and roast in the oven until an instant-read thermometer inserted sideways into the steak registers 120°F for medium rare, 6 to 8 minutes.

3. Meanwhile, add the shallots to the skillet and cook until brown and tender, about 2 minutes. Add the wine and broth and use a wooden spoon to scrape up any brown bits still left in the pan. Bring to a boil and cook about 2 minutes to let the shallots flavor the wine. Remove from the heat and whisk in the cold butter a piece at a time to make a glossy sauce. Season with salt and black pepper. Set aside and keep warm.

4. Transfer the steak to a cutting board and let rest for 10 minutes. Cut steak from the bone and slice across the grain.

red onion vs. shallot

TIPS

shopsmart
Shallots look like small, bulb-shaped, orangey-red onions. Look for smooth-skinned shallots with no black spots or sprouts coming out the top. Sometimes shallots will be split into two bulbs. If you've got a monster-size shallot, think of each bulb as one. They're mellow-tasting enough that you can eat them raw if you like, but they're also great in sauces. If you can't find them, use ¼ of a red onion.

cook's note
Here it makes sense to use a regular pan (that is, not nonstick) because that'll give you all the crusty little brown bits that flavor the sauce. Stainless steel works, as would cast iron.

sunday beef pot roast serves 4 to 6 • prep time: 2 hours 30 minutes

2   medium onions
6   cloves garlic
8   sprigs fresh parsley
8   sprigs fresh thyme
2   bay leaves
2   tablespoons vegetable oil
     Flour
1   boneless beef chuck roast
     (about 3½ to 4 pounds)
     Kosher salt and freshly ground
     black pepper
1   cup red wine
1   15-ounce can whole peeled
     tomatoes
4   medium carrots
2   ribs celery
1¼ pounds medium red potatoes

chuck roast

1. Preheat the oven to 325°F. Halve the onions, peel and slice. Smash and peel garlic. Tie parsley, thyme, and bay leaves together with a piece of kitchen string.

▶ know-how 99, 103

2. Heat the oil in a large Dutch oven with a tight-fitting lid over medium-high heat. Spread flour out on a plate or piece of waxed paper. Season the beef generously with salt and black pepper, then roll in the flour. Shake off the excess flour and add to the pan. Sear the meat, uncovered, turning until all sides are well browned, 10 to 12 minutes. Use tongs to transfer the beef to a plate.

3. Add the onions and garlic and cook, stirring, until lightly browned, about 5 minutes. Add the wine and boil until syrupy, about 3 minutes, using a wooden spoon to scrape up the brown bits that cling to the pan. Add the tomatoes to the pot, crushing them by hand as you add them. Season with salt and black pepper. Return the beef to the pot, nestling it in the tomatoes and onions, and add just enough water to cover meat ¾ of the way. Tuck the herb bundle into the liquid, cover, and bring to a simmer. Transfer to the oven and cook until the meat is just tender, about 1½ hours.

4. Once the meat is just tender, cut the carrots and celery into 2-inch chunks. Quarter the potatoes. Remove pot from the oven and scatter the vegetables around the meat into the liquid. Continue cooking the pot roast in the oven, uncovered, until the beef and vegetables are very tender, about 40 minutes. Remove and discard the herb bundle. Season the broth with salt and black pepper to taste. Remove meat and tent with foil on a cutting board to rest for 10 minutes before slicing.

▶ know-how 100

5. Arrange the vegetables on a platter. Slice the meat against the grain and add it to the platter. Spoon some of the broth over the meat and pour the rest into a small pitcher or bowl to serve at the table.

braising wisdom

• One of the major rewards of braising—besides fall-apart-tender meat—is the cooking liquid. It's delicious tossed with pasta, as a sauce for burgers, stirred into risotto, or as gravy for mashed potatoes.
• If you prefer your broth thicker and saucier, scatter a couple of tablespoons of flour over the onions while they soften before you add the wine.

TIPS

shopsmart
Marbled meat—that is, meat with a pattern of fat running through it—is full of flavor and very tender.

broiled lamb chops with lemon & fresh herbs
serves 4 • prep time: 25 minutes

1 clove garlic
6 sprigs fresh rosemary
2 lemons
½ cup extra-virgin olive oil
1 teaspoon kosher salt, plus
   additional for seasoning
   Freshly ground black pepper
8 6-ounce loin lamb chops
   Handful fresh mint, basil, or
   parsley leaves

loin lamb chop

1. Crush the garlic and bruise the rosemary with the flat side of a large knife. Juice the lemons into a dish large enough to hold the lamb chops in a single layer. Stir in the rosemary, garlic, olive oil, 1 teaspoon of the salt, and some black pepper. Trim off and discard any large flaps of fat from the lamb chops. Add the lamb, turning to coat with the marinade. Let marinate for about 15 minutes at room temperature.

▶ know-how 99, 103, 104

2. Position a broiler pan on a rack 4 to 6 inches from the broiler and preheat broiler to high while the lamb marinates.

3. Remove chops from the marinade, pat dry, and season with salt and black pepper. Carefully lay the chops on the hot broiler pan and broil, turning once halfway through cooking time, about 8 minutes for rare, 9 minutes for medium, or 10 minutes for well done. Transfer to a cutting board or platter and let rest for 5 minutes.

4. Pour the marinade into a small saucepan and bring to a boil over high heat. Boil marinade for 2 to 3 minutes to kill any bacteria that may be present from the raw meat. Pick out the rosemary and discard. Chop the herbs and stir into the sauce. Season the sauce to taste with salt and black pepper.

5. Divide the chops among 4 plates and drizzle with the sauce.

upgrades
Stir a handful of chopped black olives into the sauce along with the chopped herbs.

marinade wisdom
• Marinades tenderize and flavor poultry and meat. They can be made out of any number of ingredients; most crucial is something acidic (like lemon juice, vinegar, or yogurt) or tropical fruit (like papayas, pineapples, or kiwi). Both acids and the enzymes found in tropical fruit react with meat protein to tenderize.
• It's important to not overmarinate food; leaving food in marinade too long turns meat to mush. Marinate food in the fridge, 4 to 6 hours for smaller cuts and 12 for larger ones—never more than a day. Resealable plastic bags are great for this—put all the ingredients in, seal it, and shake.
•Make your own marinades: use a homemade or storebought dressing; mix up a combination of yogurt, herbs, and spices; or add flavorings to pineapple or papaya juice.
• Don't reuse marinades. If you're going to save the leftover marinade to make sauce, boil it first to kill any lurking bacteria.
• Let marinated ingredients come to room temperature out of the marinade before you cook them. Brush off the extra marinade before grilling or sautéing.

TIPS **cook's note**
Bruising herbs releases their flavor while keeping them in one piece.

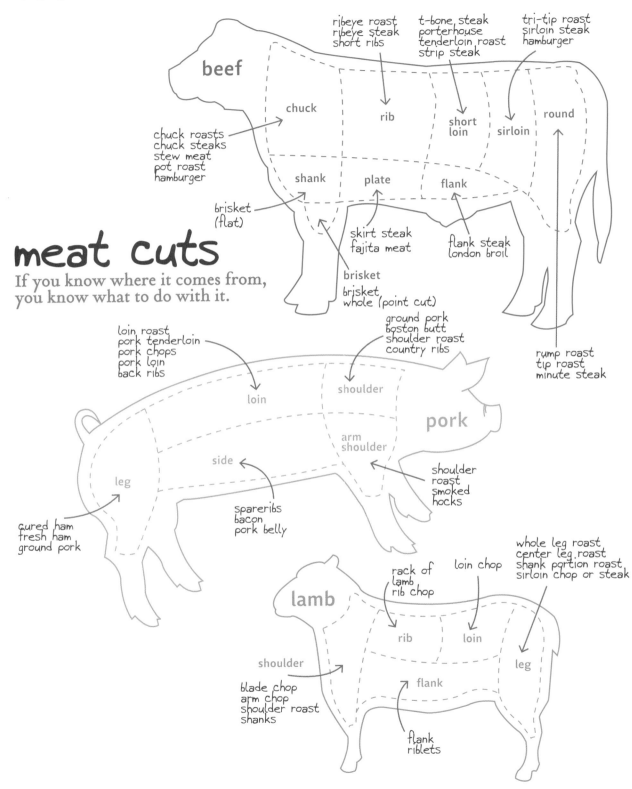

meat cuts

If you know where it comes from, you know what to do with it.

beef

ribeye roast
ribeye steak
short ribs

t-bone steak
porterhouse
tenderloin roast
strip steak

tri-tip roast
sirloin steak
hamburger

chuck

rib

short
loin

sirloin

round

chuck roasts
chuck steaks
stew meat
pot roast
hamburger

shank

plate

flank

brisket
(flat)

skirt steak
fajita meat

flank steak
london broil

brisket

brisket
whole (point cut)

rump roast
tip roast
minute steak

loin roast
pork tenderloin
pork chops
pork loin
back ribs

ground pork
boston butt
shoulder roast
country ribs

loin

shoulder

pork

arm
shoulder

side

shoulder
roast
smoked
hocks

leg

spareribs
bacon
pork belly

cured ham
fresh ham
ground pork

lamb

rack of
lamb
rib chop

loin chop

whole leg roast
center leg roast
shank portion roast
sirloin chop or steak

rib

loin

leg

shoulder

flank

blade chop
arm chop
shoulder roast
shanks

flank
riblets

lost in the meat department?

Here's an intro to the meat case **(what you need to know so you don't go home hungry). First off,** make friends **with whoever's behind the butcher counter. It'll make all of this** even easier.

When you're buying: Beef or lamb should have a rosy red color; pork should be darker colored for optimum flavor. If you're buying prepackaged, make sure the packages are tightly sealed and not leaking, and the expiration date is still valid.

In general, bone-in meat cooks up juicier than boneless. And fat's good; fat adds flavor. For steaks, fat should be on the inside (it'll have a marble pattern); for chops and roasts, on the outside.

ground (to pan-fry, grill, or stew, either loose or formed)
Cook it or freeze it; don't leave it sitting around in the fridge (2 days max). Two ounces makes a slider; 8 to 10 ounces makes a megaburger.
- beef sirloin is steakier and leaner; chuck's beefier and cheaper.
- poultry chicken or turkey should look moist and pink. Breast-only is leaner; regular is more flavorful.
- mix meatloaf mix is a combo of beef, pork, and veal; it makes excellent meatballs.

steaks, chops, and ribs (broil, pan-fry, grill, or sear 'n' roast)
Steaks and chops are both thin, quick-cooking cuts of meat. Steaks can be bone-in or boneless and are meatier tasting; chops generally have bones (either curved rib bones or T-bones) and are leaner. Plan on 6 to 10 ounces per person, depending on appetites and side dishes. We love T-boned cuts, whether beef, pork, or lamb, because they give you the best of both worlds: the tenderness of tenderloin and the meatiness of loin.
- thin steaks for weeknight dinners: look for flank steak, skirt steak, or tri-tip.
- thick steaks for special occasions: strip steak, T-bone, porterhouse, and tenderloin.
- pork chops T-bone chops are lean and flavorful; rib chops are tender and meaty.
- lamb chops rib chops are super-luxe; t-boned loin chops are tender and mild; shoulder chops are chewy and flavorful.
- boneless chops also called cutlets; good for grilling or a quick pan-fry.
- ribs kind of like mini chops. Baby back ribs are smaller and quicker cooking than spare ribs.

roasts (roast, sear 'n' roast, or braise)
A roast is a large cut of meat, either bone-in or out. It takes longer to cook than steaks, chops, or ground and is perfect for a crowd. Figure about 8 ounces a person.
- lean roasts (like pork loin) should be roasted.
- not-so-lean roasts (like beef chuck roast or pork shoulder) should be braised.

pork tenderloin (gets its own category)
It's good grilled, roasted, seared & roasted, pan-fried, or braised. Don't know what to make? Make a pork tenderloin.

pork chops with peach chutney serves 4 • prep time: 30 minutes

peach chutney

1	shallot or ¼ small onion
1	1-inch piece fresh ginger
½	lemon
3	tablespoons peach or apricot jam or preserves
1	cinnamon stick
¼	teaspoon kosher salt
	Pinch crushed red pepper flakes
1	1-pound bag frozen peaches, thawed
2	tablespoons dried cherries
1	teaspoon whole-grain mustard
	Handful fresh mint leaves

chops

4	center-cut, bone-in rib pork chops (about 10 ounces each)
	Kosher salt
	Freshly ground black pepper
2	tablespoons vegetable oil
2	tablespoons unsalted butter

1. Preheat oven to 350°F. For the chutney: Chop the shallot. Peel and chop the ginger. Juice the lemon into a medium microwave-safe bowl. Stir in the shallot, ginger, preserves, cinnamon stick, salt, and red pepper flakes. Cover and seal with plastic wrap and microwave on HIGH for 1 minute. Carefully remove the plastic wrap and stir in the peaches and cherries. Cover and microwave on HIGH for 2 minutes more. Carefully poke holes in the plastic wrap to release the steam and set aside. When slightly cool, stir in mustard and cool completely. Just before serving, chop the mint and stir into the chutney.

▶ know-how 99, 104, 103

2. Preheat a large, ovenproof skillet over medium-high heat for about 1 minute. Pat the chops dry. Season all over with salt and some black pepper. Add the oil to the skillet and heat until shimmering.

Add the chops and cook until the chops are browned, 3 to 4 minutes. Add the butter and cook for 1 minute more. Turn and continue cooking, about 4 minutes more. Transfer the skillet to the oven and cook until firm and an instant-read thermometer inserted sideways into the chop registers 140°F, 2 to 4 minutes. Transfer chops to a plate, tent with foil, and set aside to rest for 3 to 4 minutes before serving with the chutney.

searing wisdom

Depending upon the size of the chops, you may need to sear the chops in two batches in your skillet. If so, divide the oil and butter evenly for use in each batch. After searing the first batch—but before transferring them all to the oven—set the chops aside. Wipe out the skillet, heat reserved oil or butter, add the second set of chops, and cook as you did the first batch. Then transfer all the chops to the oven to finish.

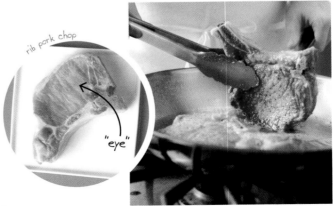

rib pork chop

"eye"

chopsmart

TIPS Choose rib chops with a good-size "eye," like the one above. If you think about rib chops as being shaped like the letter P, the eye is the semicircular part on top.

grilled pork tenderloin with quick cabbage slaw
serves 4 • prep time: 1 to 4 hours (much of it unattended)

pork

4	cloves garlic
1	cup cold water
3	tablespoons kosher salt, plus more for seasoning
2	tablespoons dark brown sugar
½	cup dark rum (optional)
2	pork tenderloins, about 12 ounces each
1	tablespoon olive oil
2	teaspoons ground cumin
	Freshly ground black pepper

quick cabbage slaw

½	medium red onion
½	head napa cabbage
	Large handful fresh cilantro
1	navel orange
2	tablespoons extra-virgin olive oil
1	tablespoon white wine vinegar
1½	teaspoons kosher salt
	Freshly ground black pepper

napa cabbage

1. To brine the pork: Smash the garlic. Combine the water, 3 tablespoons salt, brown sugar, and garlic in a medium saucepan. Bring to a boil, remove from heat, and stir in the rum, if using. Cool to room temperature.

▶ know-how 99

2. Put the tenderloins in a bowl or shallow container and pour the brine over them. (Or put the tenderloins and brine in a large resealable plastic bag.) Cover and refrigerate at least 1 hour or up to 4 hours.

3. For the slaw: Thinly slice the onion and soak it in cold water for 10 minutes, then drain and pat dry. Slice the cabbage very thinly crosswise; you should get about 6 cups. Coarsely chop the cilantro. Toss the onion, cabbage, and cilantro together in a large bowl.

▶ know-how 99, 103

4. Finely grate ½ of the orange's zest into the slaw. Cut remaining peel and white pith off the orange. Quarter and then cut the orange segments crosswise into small pieces; toss into the vegetables. Dress the slaw with olive oil, vinegar, 1½ teaspoons salt, and black pepper to taste.

▶ know-how 104

5. Preheat oven to 425° F. Heat a grill pan over medium-high heat. Brush the tenderloins with the olive oil and sprinkle with cumin and black pepper. Grill the tenderloins 5 minutes per side, then transfer to the oven and cook for an additional 10 minutes. (An instant-read thermometer should register 145°F when inserted in the thickest part of the meat.) Alternatively, broil the tenderloins: Position a rack closest to the broiler and heat to high. Lay the pork on a small shallow pan and broil until golden brown, turning once, about 5 minutes per side.

6. Set meat on a cutting board to rest for 5 minutes before slicing. Serve with the slaw.

brine wisdom

• A brine is a solution of salt, sugar, and liquid (usually water) that makes lean meat (like pork, turkey, or shrimp) juicier and more tender. Brines are different from marinades; while marinades break down fibers in meat, brines make meat juicier. Experiment with brines, adding spices, herbs, or other flavorings at will.
• The smaller the piece of meat, the shorter the brining time. You can brine a pork tenderloin for up to 4 hours; don't brine shrimp for more than half an hour.

TIPS

shopsmart
Napa cabbage, sometimes called Chinese cabbage, is mildly flavored and full of vitamin A. Look for compact, closed heads—also, the darker the leaves, the more nutritious.

cook's note
Brining is optional. If you skip it, rub the outside of the meat with chili powder (or your favorite rub) for extra flavor and take care not to overcook.

roast pork loin with apples serves 4 to 6 • prep time: 1 hour 20 minutes

1	tablespoon vegetable oil	3	medium carrots	4	tablespoons cold unsalted butter
1	boneless center-cut pork loin roast, trimmed and tied (about 2 pounds) Kosher salt and freshly ground black pepper	3	ribs celery	2	tablespoons cider vinegar
		3	cloves garlic	1	cup apple cider
		2	crisp, tart apples, such as Jonathan or Cortland	2	tablespoons whole-grain mustard
		3	sprigs fresh thyme		
1	medium onion	3	sprigs fresh rosemary		

1. Preheat oven to 400°F. In a large ovenproof skillet heat the vegetable oil over high heat. Season the pork loin generously with salt and black pepper. Sear the meat until golden brown on all sides, 2 to 3 minutes per side.

2. Meanwhile, thickly slice onion. Cut each carrot and celery rib into 4 chunks. Smash and peel the garlic. Peel and core the apples and cut into 8 slices each.

▶ know-how 99, 100

3. Transfer the meat to a plate. Add onion, carrots, celery, garlic, herb sprigs, and 2 tablespoons of the butter to the skillet. Cook until the vegetables are browned, about 8 minutes, stirring occasionally.

Stir in the sliced apples, then push the mixture to the sides and place the pork loin in the middle of the skillet along with any collected juices from the plate. Transfer the skillet to the oven and roast until an instant-read thermometer inserted into the center of the pork registers 145°F to 150°F, 35 to 40 minutes.

4. Transfer the pork to a cutting board and cover loosely with foil while you make the sauce. Arrange the apples and vegetables on a serving platter. Remove and discard the herb sprigs. Return the skillet to high heat and add the vinegar, scraping the bottom with a wooden spoon to loosen any browned bits. Boil until vinegar is syrupy and

reduced by half. Add the cider and reduce by about half again. Take the skillet off the heat and whisk in the mustard, then whisk in the remaining 2 tablespoons cold butter. Season with salt and black pepper.

5. Cut the strings from the pork if needed. Slice about 1/2 inch thick and arrange slices over the apple mixture. Drizzle some sauce over meat and serve the rest on the side.

apple wisdom

· Use crisp apples for cooking. They retain their shape and don't end up as applesauce.
· Apple cider is unfiltered apple juice—it's thicker, tangier, and more appley-tasting than juice. Because it's unfiltered it's got a cloudy look to it; that's totally normal.

TIPS
cook's note
If you cook your pork this way, it'll still be pink on the inside. It's perfectly fine to eat, but if you don't want pink, cook it to 160°F. It'll still be tasty, but not quite as juicy.

chinese lacquered baby back ribs

4 main course servings, up to 8 for party finger food • prep time: about 2½ hours

2	racks baby back ribs (about 2 pounds total)
1	3-inch piece fresh ginger
5	cloves garlic
1	cup rice vinegar

¼	cup soy sauce
1	tablespoon dark sesame oil
	Kosher salt
	Freshly ground black pepper
1	teaspoon five-spice powder (optional)
½	cup hoisin sauce

3	to 4 teaspoons Asian chili sauce, such as Sriracha or sambal oelek
1	tablespoon water
4	scallions
1	teaspoon sesame seeds, for garnish (optional)

1. Remove the inside membrane from the ribs. Roughly chop the ginger to get about ½ cup. Smash, peel, and roughly chop the garlic. Whisk the ginger, garlic, vinegar, soy sauce, and sesame oil in a nonreactive dish (see Cook's Note, below). Add the ribs, turning to coat evenly. Cover and refrigerate for 1 hour.

▶ know-how 99

2. Preheat the oven to 350°F. Remove the ribs from the marinade, brush off the ginger and garlic, and discard the marinade. Pat dry and season on all sides with salt, black pepper and the five-spice powder, if using. Place the ribs, bone side up, on a rimmed baking sheet and cover the sheet tightly with foil. Bake for 45 minutes.

3. Whisk the hoisin sauce, chili sauce, and water in a small bowl. Remove the ribs from the oven and brush all over with the sauce. Cook uncovered, meat side up, until the ribs are tender and nicely glazed, 30 to 35 minutes.

4. Transfer the ribs to a cutting board and let rest 5 minutes. Thinly slice the white and green parts of the scallions. Cut between the rib bones and place ribs on a serving platter. Scatter scallions and sesame seeds, if using, on top.

▶ know-how 99

removing membrane from baby back ribs

sambal oelek

 cook's note
A nonreactive dish is basically any dish not made out of aluminum.

shopsmart
• Five-spice powder is a Chinese spice mix containing more or less equal parts of cinnamon, cloves, fennel seeds, star anise, and Szechwan peppercorn, ground together to a fine powder.

• Hoisin sauce is a thick, rich, and sweet bean-based sauce. Look for it in an Asian market if you can't find it in the international aisle of your store. It's good brushed onto steaks, pork chops, or hamburgers before grilling or as a condiment for Asian noodle dishes.
• Asian chile sauces like sambal oelek are an easy way to add a quick hit of fire to a dish. Look for them packaged in jars in the international aisle of your store and keep them in the fridge once open; they last forever.

fish

It's easy to cook and ridiculously good for you. We'll give you the basics; you give it a shot.

shrimp with tomatoes, basil & garlic **181** oven-roasted salmon with lemon-dill seasoned salt **182** pan-fried salmon with cucumber-radish salad **182** mexican fish & chips **184** spicy pecan fish **185** grilled tuna with mojo **187**

fish wisdom

The easiest way to think about fish is to divide it into two categories, finfish and shellfish:

finfish
- Lean fish (like flounder, cod, mahi mahi, grouper, scrod, or haddock) are generally white fleshed, mild tasting, and low-cal.
- Oily fish (salmon, fresh tuna, trout, or mackerel) have a richer taste and darker flesh and are packed with omega-3 acids (good for your heart).

shellfish
- Crustaceans: Shrimp are best bought frozen. Peeled, cooked frozen shrimp are amazingly convenient. Lobster and crab are best bought live.
- Bivalves (like mussels or clams) should also be bought live, with intact, closed shells (they open up when you cook them).

shopping
- Be choosy; when you're buying fillets—check them out: They should be firm, look moist, and smell like the ocean.
- Be flexible; always buy what looks best at the store, even if it's not necessarily what your recipe calls for. If it's roughly similar (like another mild white-fleshed fish), you're good to go.
- Be demanding; ask for center-cut fish (not tail pieces), or buy a whole fish and ask your fishmonger to filet it.
- Be considerate; check online (or ask your fishmonger) which fish are the environmentally smart ones to choose and pick the abundant ones.

storing
- Buy fish the day you plan to cook it and keep it in the coldest part of the fridge (all the way in the back). Or keep it on ice in a colander set in a bowl, which should keep it good for a day or two. Freezing fish makes it a little mushy; fine for broiling or stews, not great for sautés.

cooking
- If the smell freaks you out, stick to lean fish or try cooking it mostly in the oven. Broiling's the easiest way to cook any fish.
- If you think fish is too fishy tasting, cook it less. The less you cook fish, the richer and butterier it tastes (the longer, the stronger). You're best off undercooking it slightly; the residual heat will finish it off.
- Don't cook fish until it flakes (it'll be overdone). Cook it for 6 minutes per inch of thickness; it's done at an internal temperature of 135°F.

shrimp with tomatoes, basil & garlic
serves 4 • prep time: 15 minutes

1½ cups cherry or grape tomatoes
(about ¾ of a pint container)
Handful of fresh basil leaves

¾ teaspoon kosher salt, plus more
for seasoning
Freshly ground black pepper
1 large clove garlic

1¼ pounds peeled and deveined
medium or large shrimp
2 tablespoons extra-virgin olive
oil or unsalted butter
1 lemon

1. Halve or quarter the tomatoes if large. Tear or roughly chop the basil leaves. Toss the tomatoes and basil in a medium bowl and season with the salt and some black pepper. Set aside so the tomatoes get juicy. Smash, peel, and mince the garlic.

▶ know-how 99

2. Spread the shrimp out on a clean pan or cutting board and pat them completely dry with a paper towel. Heat a large skillet over high heat. Season the shrimp with some salt and black pepper. Add a little less than half the olive oil or butter to the skillet. Lay half the shrimp

in the pan relatively quickly so they cook evenly. Cook the shrimp, undisturbed, until they turn golden brown on the bottom, about 2 minutes. Add a bit more oil and scatter half the garlic in the skillet. Turn the heat off and turn the shrimp over with tongs. Cook for 1 minute in the residual heat of the skillet. Transfer the shrimp to the bowl with the tomato mixture and toss to combine. Reheat the pan and repeat with the remaining oil, shrimp, and garlic.

3. Cut the lemon into wedges. Divide the shrimp among 4 plates or mound on a serving platter. Serve, with the lemon wedges, hot or at room temperature.

make it your own
Instead of basil, try dill, parsley, or mint. Toss over pasta.

shrimp wisdom
· Shrimp really don't need tons of heat; too much can turn them tough. The pan's still going to be hot after you turn the burner off—just hot enough to cook the shrimp through without toughening them up.
· Shrimp cook so fast that it's key to get all of them in the pan at once so they cook evenly. If you crowd the pan, they won't brown, so do a layer at a time.

TIPS

shopsmart
Big bags of uncooked frozen shrimp are great to have in the freezer—they defrost superfast, so you'll always have something to eat.

cook's note
You should be able to buy shrimp already deveined; if not, use a paring knife to make a cut down the outside of the curve of the shrimp, then pull out the thin gray vein you find.

oven-roasted salmon with lemon-dill seasoned salt
serves 4 • prep time: 25 minutes

1 lemon
 Several sprigs fresh dill, plus
  more for garnish
1 tablespoon kosher salt
1 heaping teaspoon sugar
 Pinch cayenne pepper
4 6-ounce center-cut salmon
  fillets with skin
 Vegetable oil, for brushing the
  salmon

1. Preheat the oven to 300°F. Line a rimmed baking sheet with foil. Zest half the lemon into a small bowl. (Save zested lemon, wrapped and refrigerated, for another use.) Finely chop the dill, about 1 tablespoon in all, and add to the bowl. Stir in the salt, sugar, and cayenne pepper.

know-how 103, 104

2. Lightly brush the salmon with vegetable oil. Evenly sprinkle the spiced salt over the top (but not the sides) of the fillets and place on the baking sheet, skin side up. Roast until the bottom is glazed, the sides are opaque, and the salmon is just cooked through, about 18 minutes. Transfer the salmon to serving plates with a metal spatula or pancake turner. Add a sprig of dill to each and serve.

pan-fried salmon with cucumber-radish salad
serves 4 • prep time: 20 to 25 minutes

4 6-ounce center-cut salmon
  fillets (about 1 inch thick),
  with or without skin
2 teaspoons sesame seeds
1 English cucumber or 2 regular
4 to 5 radishes
½ jalapeño
1 1-inch piece fresh ginger
2 tablespoons vegetable oil
1 tablespoon rice vinegar
 Pinch sugar
1 teaspoon kosher salt, plus more
  for seasoning
¼ teaspoon dark sesame oil
 Freshly ground black pepper

1. Bring salmon to room temperature 10 minutes before cooking. Toast the sesame seeds in a small dry skillet over medium heat, stirring and tossing, until fragrant and a shade or two darker, about 4 minutes. Pour into a small bowl to cool.

2. Meanwhile, quarter the cucumber lengthwise and thinly slice crosswise. (If using regular waxed cucumbers, peel and seed them first.) Put in a medium bowl. Trim and discard radish tops if needed, then thinly slice the radishes and add to cucumbers. Stem, seed, and finely chop the jalapeño. Peel the ginger and finely grate using a rasp or fine-hole grater to yield about 1 teaspoon.

Add jalapeño and ginger to the salad and toss. Add 1 tablespoon of the oil, the toasted sesame seeds, vinegar, sugar, 1 teaspoon salt, and the sesame oil. Toss the salad and set aside.

know-how 102, 99

3. Heat a large skillet over medium-low heat. Season salmon with some salt and black pepper. Add remaining 1 tablespoon vegetable oil to the pan; raise heat to medium high. Place salmon, skin side up, in the pan. Cook, without moving fish, until golden brown, about 4 minutes. Turn fillets over with a metal spatula and cook until fish feels firm to the touch, about 3 minutes more. Transfer to plates or a platter and serve warm with cucumber salad.

shopsmart
TIPS There's a lot of salmon out there. What you need to know: Wild salmon is deep red in color and more salmony-tasting (in a good way). Farmed salmon is pinker, milder, and substantially cheaper. If you love salmon, and can get wild, go for it.

mexican fish & chips serves 4 • prep time: 30 minutes

2 tablespoons extra-virgin olive oil

1 7-ounce can salsa verde (tomatillo salsa) (about ¾ cup)

3 scallions
Large handful tortilla chips

½ cup crumbled feta cheese

4 6-ounce skinless mahi mahi or grouper fillets
Kosher salt and freshly ground black pepper
Handful fresh cilantro

1. Preheat the oven to 450°F. Heat 1 tablespoon of the olive oil in a medium skillet over medium-high heat. Add the salsa and cook, stirring, until thickened, about 3 minutes. Pour salsa into a 9x13-inch baking dish and cool slightly.

2. Slice the scallions. Crumble the tortilla chips by hand in a medium bowl to yield about ⅔ cup. Mix with the scallions, cheese, and remaining tablespoon olive oil.

▶ know-how 99

3. Lightly season each fish fillet with some salt and black pepper. Turn fish in the salsa to coat and arrange, skinned side down, in the pan. Pat the chip mixture evenly on top of fish.

4. Bake until fish is opaque and topping is lightly browned, about 20 minutes. Chop cilantro, sprinkle over fish, and serve immediately.

upgrade
Sprinkle ¼ cup chopped green Spanish olives over the salsa verde.

make it your own
If you can find it, try a Mexican cheese in place of feta. Queso blanco (fresh, firm, creamy), queso fresco (semisoft, salty, not too melty), or cotija añejo (crumbly, dry, strong) all work well here. Leftover Oaxaca and queso fresco are excellent in quesadillas and burritos, or crumble cotija or queso blanco over soup or chili.

salsa verde

queso fresco

cotija añejo

queso blanco

oaxaca

shopsmart
TIPS Salsa verde is made with tomatillos, which look like green tomatoes with papery husks. Though they're not actually related to tomatoes, they still make excellent (tangy, bright-tasting) salsa.

spicy pecan fish serves 4 • prep time: 15 minutes

- 5 tablespoons unsalted butter
- ¼ cup all-purpose flour
- ½ teaspoon chili powder
- 1 teaspoon kosher salt, plus more for seasoning
- 4 6-ounce skinless scrod or haddock fillets
- ⅓ cup pecans
- 5 fresh sage leaves
- 3 tablespoons cider vinegar
- 1 teaspoon honey
- ½ teaspoon hot pepper sauce
  Freshly ground black pepper

1. Position a rack 4 to 6 inches from the broiler and preheat broiler. Melt the butter in a small skillet and lightly brush a baking dish with some of the butter.

2. Mix the flour and chili powder together on a plate. Season the fish with the 1 teaspoon salt and roll in the seasoned flour to coat. Shake off the excess flour and place the fish in a single layer, skinned side down, in the prepared baking dish. Drizzle another tablespoon or so of the butter over the fish. Broil the fish until firm to the touch, 8 to 10 minutes.

3. Meanwhile, roughly chop the pecans and sage. Cook the pecans in the remaining butter over medium heat, swirling the pan occasionally, until they are toasted and fragrant, about 5 minutes. Remove skillet from the heat and let cool slightly. Carefully whisk in the cider vinegar, honey, hot sauce, and sage. (Be careful—the butter may foam and bubble when you add the liquids.) Season with salt and black pepper to taste. Put the fish on serving plates, pour the pecans and butter over the fish, and serve.

5 minutes

2 minutes

4 minutes

TIPS

cook's note

Browned-butter sauces are one of the best things that ever happened to fish. When you heat butter, the milk solids burn slightly, giving the butter a toasty brown color and a nutty, rich taste. It can go from brown to black in seconds, though, so be sure to stand there and watch it as it cooks.

shopsmart

Scrod, despite the urban legend to the contrary, isn't a made-up word for "catch of the day"—it's young cod.

grilled tuna with mojo serves 4 • prep time: 30 minutes

mojo

4	cloves garlic
½	to 1 small fresh jalapeño or serrano chile

	Handful fresh cilantro
4	limes
¼	cup extra-virgin olive oil
1	teaspoon kosher salt

tuna

2	12-ounce tuna steaks (about 1¼ inches thick)
1	tablespoon extra-virgin olive oil
	Heaping ½ teaspoon kosher salt
	Freshly ground black pepper

1. Heat an outdoor grill or a stovetop grill pan to medium-high.

2. For the mojo: Smash, peel, and chop the garlic. Halve the chile lengthwise and remove the stem. For a milder mojo, scrape out the seeds with the tip of your knife; for maximum heat, leave the seeds in. Slice the chile very thinly. Coarsely chop the cilantro. Juice the limes.
▶ know-how 99, 103, 104

3. Stir the garlic and olive oil together in a medium microwave-safe bowl, cover loosely with plastic wrap, and microwave on HIGH until the garlic is soft and aromatic, about 2 minutes. Add the chile, lime juice, cilantro, and salt to the hot oil. Set aside to cool until ready to serve.

4. For the tuna: Brush the tuna with olive oil and season generously with the salt and some black pepper. Grill until there are distinct grill marks on both sides, turning once, 3 to 5 minutes per side for medium rare or 4 to 6 minutes for cooked through. (If cooking on an outdoor grill, the fire should be hotter than a grill pan, so use the shorter cooking times.) Let rest for 5 minutes.

5. Slice each tuna steak in half, divide among plates, and drizzle with some of the mojo, passing more at the table.

grilling wisdom
Grill pans are fantastic if you can't grill outdoors. If you don't have one, use a flat, heavy-bottomed pan.

shopsmart
TIPS
When you're buying tuna steaks, look for moist, shiny, pinkish red flesh, and go as thick as you can. It's harder to overcook a thick steak (tuna really, really hates being overcooked). If you're going to serve it rare, like we do, make sure your tuna's the best quality (sometimes referred to as sushi-grade).

beans & grains

The ultimate no-effort food: a tasty, filling meal you can feel good about.

beans & grains of wisdom

beans

beans

- Black, white, and red beans come either canned (fully cooked) or dried (raw) and taste meaty and rich even though they're low fat.
- Most dried beans need to be soaked, either overnight in cold water or quick-soaked: Cover them with water, bring the water to a boil, then turn off the heat and let stand for an hour. Drain, rinse, and you're good to go. Beans should always be thoroughly cooked; they're not supposed to be al dente. Canned beans are ready to eat and just need a quick rinse before using.

lentils

- Lentils are quick-cooking (30 minutes or less) and don't need to be soaked. The most common kind are a khaki color, which might be called green or brown, depending on the packaging. Other varieties include French green lentils, red lentils, yellow lentils, and black lentils.

tofu

- Tofu's a bean, sort of. It's made from soybeans and comes in firm, soft, and silken forms, all available in individually wrapped blocks (usually found in the refrigerated section of the supermarket). Firm tofu is great for high-heat stir-fries, and soft and silken tofu tend to be better with more gentle cooking.

grains

rice

- Rice can be long-grained, short-grained, fat, thin, white, brown, black, or red. Long-grain rice is mildly flavored, fluffy and soft. Short-grain rice is flavorful and stickier than long-grain. Basmati rice is also long-grained, though it's more aromatic and flavorful and less soft than regular long-grain. Arborio rice is short, fat, and turns creamy when cooked, making it perfect for risotto. Brown rice can be any kind of rice. It's less processed than white rice and has a nutty flavor and chewy texture. It's always better (in terms of both cost and taste) to buy rice in bulk.

polenta

- Polenta is a kind of coarsely ground cornmeal. If you live in the South, you'll recognize it as not that different from grits. Quick-cooking polenta (the box kind, not the tube kind) speeds up the prep time without compromising too much on flavor. It can be cooked so that it sets up either creamy or firm.

bulgur

- Bulgur is partially cooked, dried cracked wheat. It's nutty tasting, low fat, and high fiber.

storage

- Keep rice and other grains in tightly sealed plastic containers in the cupboard or in the freezer if you don't use them that often. Lentils, dried beans, and canned beans all belong in the cupboard as well, and tofu's best wrapped in plastic in the fridge.

basic long-grain white rice
(all purpose—sides, salads, fried rice. if a recipe just calls for rice, this is probably what you need.)

brown rice
(has only the husk removed in milling; it is a little sticky, chewy, and has a nutty aroma and flavor. it can come either long grain or short. long is fluffier and short is chewy.)

basmati
(use as an accompaniment to indian curries or as a more flavorful substitute for long-grain rice)

rice variety	rice	liquid	salt	butter or oil	method (serves 2 to 4)
basic white rice	1 cup	1 ¼ cups water	½ tsp.	2 tsp.	Put water, salt, rice, and butter or oil in a medium saucepan with tight-fitting lid. Bring to full boil. Stir with fork; reduce to simmer. Cover; cook 18 minutes without disturbing pot, peeking, or stirring. Set off the heat 5 minutes (again, no peeking). Fluff and serve.
toasted rice pilaf	1 cup	1 ¼ cups water or broth	½ tsp.	2 tsp.	Cook rice in the butter or oil (uncovered in saucepan with tight-fitting lid), stirring until toasty, about 4 minutes. Add liquid and salt; bring to a full boil. Stir with fork; reduce to simmer. Cover; cook 18 minutes, without disturbing pot or peeking. Set off the heat 5 minutes (again, no peeking). Fluff and serve.
basmati (or other long-grain rice)	1 cup	1 ¼ cups water	½ tsp.	No	Cook like basic white rice but for 15 minutes.
brown rice	1 cup	2 cups water or broth	¾ tsp.	2 tsp. butter (optional)	Put water, salt, rice, and butter, if using, in a medium saucepan with a tight-fitting lid. Bring to full boil. Stir with fork; reduce to a simmer. Cover; cook without disturbing the pot or peeking until rice is tender, 45 minutes. Set aside 10 minutes (again, no peeking). Fluff and serve.

TIPS

cook's note
Leftover rice (any kind) is a great thing to have—you can reheat it in the microwave (sprinkle it with a little water first and cover it with plastic wrap), make fried rice (stir-fry it in oil with whatever veggies you have already cooked or frozen), or toss it with veggies and a simple dressing for rice salad.

mexican rice casserole serves 4 • prep time: 45 minutes

- 1 large onion
- 4 cloves garlic
- 2 tablespoons olive oil, plus more for brushing in the baking dish
- 2 teaspoons kosher salt
- 1 teaspoon dried oregano
- 1 teaspoon ground cumin
- ¼ teaspoon freshly ground black pepper
- 12 ounces Monterey Jack cheese
- 1 14.5-ounce can diced fire-roasted tomatoes
- 1 4.5-ounce can chopped roasted green chiles
- 2 cups cooked white rice
- 1½ cups chopped or shredded cooked meat, such as chicken, chorizo, beef, or pork (optional)

1. Preheat oven to 350°F. Grease an 8x8-inch casserole with a little olive oil. Chop the onion. Smash, peel, and chop the garlic. Heat the 2 tablespoons olive oil in a large skillet over medium heat. Add the onion, garlic, salt, oregano, cumin, and black pepper. Cook, stirring occasionally, until the onion is tender, about 5 minutes.

▶ know-how 99

2. Meanwhile, dice the cheese and set aside. Add the tomatoes and chiles to the skillet, increase the heat to high, and simmer until thickened, 4 to 5 minutes.

3. Stir in the rice, cheese, and cooked meat, if using. Transfer to the prepared dish and bake until browned and bubbly, 30 to 35 minutes. Remove from the oven and let stand about 10 minutes before serving.

make it your own
Cook bell peppers, corn, or zucchini in a little olive oil and add them along with the rice or stir in some chopped cilantro or scallions before the casserole goes into the oven.

TIPS

cook's note
This casserole, like most, can be assembled and refrigerated ahead of time. If you go that route, take it out of the fridge about 30 minutes before you bake it. Letting casseroles stand out of the oven for 10 minutes or so before serving makes them a little more solid and easier to cut.

shopsmart
Canned roasted green chiles are a good bet for a mellow chile burn. Fire-roasted tomatoes give you a more concentrated tomatoey flavor with a hint of smokiness.

cheese risotto serves 4 • prep time: 30 to 35 minutes

6 cups water or half water and half chicken broth	2 tablespoons extra-virgin olive oil	2 tablespoons unsalted butter
2 teaspoons kosher salt	1½ cups Arborio rice	½ cup freshly grated Parmesan cheese, plus more for serving
1 medium onion	½ cup white wine or dry white vermouth	Freshly ground black pepper

1. Put the water (or water and broth, if using) in a medium saucepan and add the salt. Bring to barely a simmer over low heat.

2. Finely chop the onion. Heat the olive oil in a large soup pot or Dutch oven over medium heat. Add the onion and cook until tender, about 6 minutes. Add the rice and stir to lightly "toast" the rice and coat it with oil, about 2 minutes.

▶ know-how 99

3. Add the wine and cook, stirring constantly with a wooden spoon, until the rice absorbs the wine, about 2 minutes.

4. Add just enough of the hot liquid to completely moisten the rice (about 1 cup or so) and

adjust the heat so the risotto is at a brisk simmer but not boiling. Stir frequently until the rice absorbs the liquid, about 1 minute. When there is just a thin film of starchy liquid at the bottom of the skillet, add about 1 cup of liquid again. Cook, stirring, until it is absorbed. Repeat the process until the risotto is creamy but still al dente, 16 to 18 minutes. (You may not use all the liquid.)

5. Cut the butter into 4 or 5 pieces. Remove the risotto from the heat and vigorously beat in the butter. Stir in the cheese. Divide risotto among 4 warm bowls, grind a generous amount of black pepper over each, and serve, passing more cheese at the table.

upgrades

• Add another layer of flavor with good vegetable, chicken, or fish broth.
• Add a cup of cooked vegetables (asparagus, mushrooms, peas, zucchini, spinach, or artichokes), thawed frozen vegetables, or leftover roasted vegetables (beets, butternut squash, pumpkin) with the last addition of liquid. Or add a cup or two of cooked meat, poultry, or seafood.
• As you're beating in the butter, add the juice and zest of a lemon, ¼ to ⅓ cup of chopped fresh herbs, or try a different type of hard cheese.
• Use about a cup of leftover sauce or stew, adding it about ⅔ of the way through in place of some of the water. Marinara sauce is great here, as is any hearty meat- or poultry-based stew (just chop any big pieces of meat or vegetables before you add them).

toasting rice

stirring frequently

adding liquid

serving

TIPS **cook's note**
Risotto continues to cook after you take it off the heat, so even if it's still slightly underdone when you add the butter, it'll finish by the time it gets to the table.

polenta with sausage serves 4 • prep time: 20 minutes

4 cups liquid (chicken broth, milk, water, or a combination)
¾ cup quick-cooking polenta
1 tablespoon extra-virgin olive oil
4 large precooked seasoned chicken sausage links, about 13 ounces
2 cups marinara sauce, homemade (page 121) or storebought
2 tablespoons unsalted butter
    Handful fresh basil (optional)
½ cup grated grana-style cheese, such as Parmesan
½ teaspoon kosher salt
    Freshly ground black pepper

1. Put the liquid in a medium saucepan and bring to a boil over high heat. Slowly whisk in the polenta, reduce the heat to low, and cook, stirring occasionally, until the polenta is thick and creamy, about 15 minutes.

2. While the polenta simmers, heat the oil in a medium skillet over medium heat. Add the sausage and cook, turning occasionally, until it's browned on all sides, about 5 minutes. Add the marinara sauce and bring to a simmer. Let the marinara simmer while the polenta cooks.

3. Cut the butter into bits. If using the basil, wash and pat dry. Remove the polenta saucepan from the heat and whisk in ¼ cup of the cheese, the butter, salt, and some black pepper. Remove the sausage from the sauce and set aside. Tear the basil leaves, if using, into the marinara sauce and stir in remaining cheese. Immediately serve the polenta topped with the sausage and sauce.

make it your own

Top creamy polenta with crumbled blue cheese.

firmed-up polenta slices

cook's note

TIPS
If you've got leftover polenta, pour it into a loaf pan or dish. Let it cool, then refrigerate until firm. Slice it, top it with cheese, and run it under the broiler for a quick snack or side.

baked mexican black beans
serves 4 to 6 • prep time: 2½ hours

1   pound dried black beans
6   slices bacon
1   large onion
5   cloves garlic
2   teaspoons ground cumin
1   bay leaf
6   cups water, chicken broth,
     or a combination
1   jalapeño
2   teaspoons kosher salt
     Freshly ground black pepper
1   14-ounce can diced tomatoes
1   tablespoon cider vinegar

topping
1   red or yellow bell pepper
5   scallions
1   cup sour cream
½   teaspoon kosher salt
     Freshly ground black pepper

1. Preheat the oven to 350°F. Rinse the beans in a colander.

2. Cut the bacon crosswise into thin strips. Cook in a medium Dutch oven (or a soup pot with a tight-fitting lid that can go in the oven) over medium heat until almost crisp, about 10 minutes. Roughly chop the onion. Smash, peel, and chop the garlic. Stir the onion, garlic, cumin, and bay leaf into the bacon. Cook, stirring occasionally, until onion is tender, about 8 minutes.

▶ know-how 99

3. Add the beans, water, the whole jalapeño, the salt, and some black pepper. Stir with a wooden spoon to scrape up any brown bits in the pan. Bring to a boil, cover, and bake for 1 hour. Uncover, add the tomatoes and their juices, and bake until beans are tender and soupy, about 45 minutes to 1 hour. Stir in vinegar.

4. While the beans bake make the topping: Cut the sides off the pepper, chop into small pieces, and put in a medium bowl. Trim the scallions, thinly slice the white and green parts, and add to the bowl. Stir in the sour cream and season with ½ teaspoon salt and some black pepper.

▶ know-how 101, 99

upgrade
Add 1 cup roughly chopped fresh cilantro, either to the cooked beans when you stir in the vinegar or scattered over the fresh topping.

TIPS

cook's note
For a thicker bean dish, puree about half the beans in the Dutch oven with an immersion blender until creamy. Leftovers are great in burritos.

what makes a meal?

Planning an appealing, nutritious meal is nothing more than simple addition with a little attention to aesthetics thrown in.

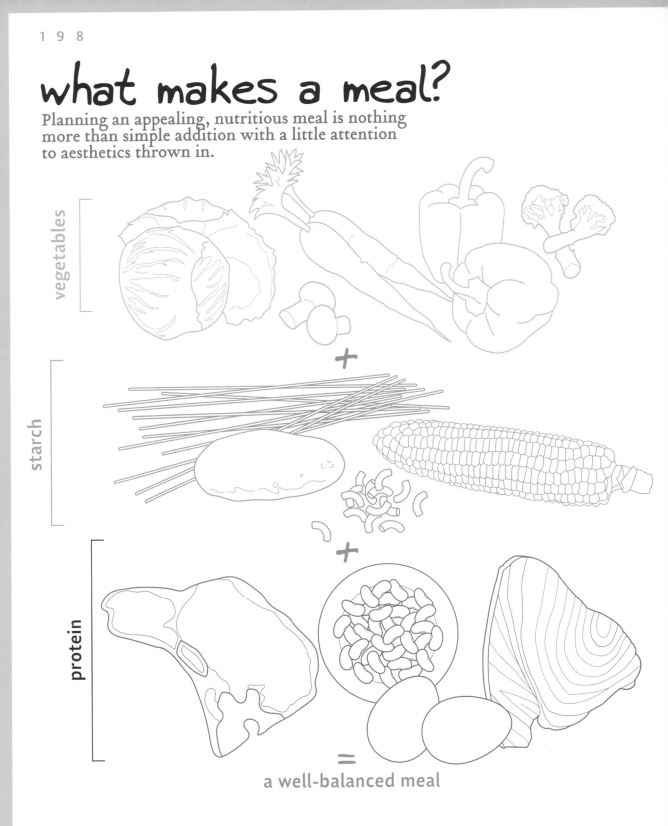

vegetables

+

starch

+

protein

=

a well-balanced meal

Really, anything's a meal, from last night's cold pizza (for breakfast) to Thanksgiving dinner. What we're trying to get at here is what makes an appealing meal.

variety's key. you want:

- A few different colors on the plate (it looks good and it's good for you)
- A few different textures (not all mushy or all crunchy)
- A few different cooking styles (not all boiled or all roasted)
- A few different foods (start with three: a vegetable, a starch, and a protein)

That said, keep it simple—try to serve sides from the same ethnic group or tradition as the main dish. You want side dishes to complement the main dish, not fight with it. Think about classic combos (rich steak and comforting potatoes, or spicy curry and mellow rice). They're classics because they hit the right balance of flavor, texture, and tradition. If you're planning a serious dessert, keep the rest of the meal light.

on the health front:

First off: It's not just what you eat, it's how much. Eat until you're full, not until you're stuffed. Protein takes many forms, from a slab of meat to a bowl of lentils, and it works equally well as a star player or in a supporting role. Set it up to support your starch and veggies—the more of your starch that comes from whole grains, the better. Round out meals with at least one vegetable, but ideally more—yeah, they're good for you, but they really can (and do) taste good. So eat them.

some sample menus

①
- Little Tomato Salad with Fresh Herbs (page 87)
- Cheese Risotto with an upgrade (page 195)
- Roasted mushrooms (page 208)
- Ice cream with Chocolate Glaze (page 234)

②
- Marinated Roasted Peppers (page 217) and Green Salad (page 80)
- Date-Night Chicken (page 142)
- Couscous with Carrots & Raisins (page 126)
- Deep-Dish Brownies (page 226) or Cheesecake (page 243) if you really want to impress

③
- Picnic Potato Salad (page 216)
- Fried Chicken (page 147)
- Roasted broccoli (page 207) (or roasted mixed veggies, see pages 207-209) or Wilted Spinach (page 210)
- 2-by-4 Fruit Salad (page 231)

④
- Smoothie (it's a meal in a glass) (page 22)

middle eastern lentil & rice pilaf
serves 4 • prep time: 40 minutes

1   **large onion**
⅓   **cup extra-virgin olive oil, plus**
      2 tablespoons
1   **teaspoon kosher salt**
      Freshly ground black pepper
2   **cloves garlic**
½   **cup long-grain white rice**
½   **cup green (aka brown)**
      lentils
½   **teaspoon ground allspice**
3   **cups water**
1   **large lemon**

for serving:
½   **cup Greek-style yogurt, for**
      serving (optional)

lentils

1. Halve, peel, and thinly slice the onion. Heat ⅓ cup olive oil in a large skillet over medium heat. Add the onion and cook, stirring occasionally, until it is tender and golden brown, 30 to 45 minutes (or more, see photos below), adjusting the heat as needed if the onion starts to brown too quickly. Season with ½ teaspoon of the salt and some black pepper.

▶ know-how 99

2. Meanwhile, smash and peel the garlic. Heat the remaining olive oil in a Dutch oven over medium-high heat. Add rice and stir to coat. Cook, stirring occasionally, until rice is lightly toasted, about 5 minutes. Add the lentils, stirring to coat. Add the garlic, allspice,

and remaining ½ teaspoon salt and cook, stirring until fragrant, about 1 minute. Add the water, increase heat to high, and bring to a rolling boil. Adjust the heat to maintain a low simmer, cover, and cook until the lentils are tender and all the water has been absorbed, about 20 minutes. (No peeking.)

▶ know-how 99

3. Quarter the lemon. To serve, toss the caramelized onions with the lentils and rice and sprinkle with the juice of 1 or 2 lemon wedges or to taste. Stir and mound onto a platter. Serve with the yogurt and the additional lemon wedges to pass at the table, if desired.

brown   browner   brownest

TIPS

shopsmart
Greek-style yogurt is thick and creamy. If you can't find it, drain plain whole-milk yogurt overnight through a coffee filter or paper towel in a strainer over a bowl in the fridge, discarding the liquid that accumulates.

cook's note
Cooking onions for a long time over low heat caramelizes the sugars and turns them rich and sweet. Make extra—leftovers are great in pasta, risotto, mashed potatoes, or on top of pizza or burgers.

tabbouleh serves 4 • prep time: 35 minutes

1¼ cups water
1   cup medium-grain bulgur
2½ teaspoons salt, plus more
    for seasoning
2   large or 6 medium ripe plum
    tomatoes (about 1½ pounds)
1   bunch fresh flat-leaf parsley
1   bunch fresh mint
4   scallions
2   lemons
¼   cup extra-virgin olive oil
    Freshly ground black pepper

medium-grain bulgur

1. Bring the water to a boil in a small saucepan. Add the bulgur and ½ teaspoon of the salt. Stir and remove from the heat. Cover with a tight-fitting lid and let the bulgur sit for 30 minutes. (No peeking.)

2. Use a paring knife to cut out the core of the tomatoes and halve them crosswise. Squeeze out and discard the seeds. Chop the tomatoes into small pieces and toss in a colander with ½ teaspoon of the salt; set in the sink to drain.

▶ know-how 105

3. Hold each bunch of herbs upside down over your cutting board and shave the leaves off using a very sharp knife. Wash the leaves and dry well in a salad spinner or between paper towels. Finely chop the herbs and put in a large serving bowl.

▶ know-how 103

4. Thinly slice the white and green parts of the scallions and add to the herbs. Juice the lemons through your fingers or a strainer (to catch the seeds) into the bowl. Stir in the olive oil, remaining salt, and black pepper to taste.

▶ know-how 99, 104

5. Fluff the bulgur with a fork and add to the salad bowl. Toss in the tomatoes and use a big spoon to mix everything together evenly. Taste and season with salt and black pepper, if necessary.

upgrades
Add more veggies: Diced cucumber, sliced radishes, pitted Kalamata olives, or diced red bell pepper all work. Or add some protein: chickpeas, shredded cooked chicken, leftover salmon, crumbled feta cheese, or toasted pine nuts, almonds, or walnuts.

TIPS

a side of history
The name "tabbouleh" comes from the Arabic verb for "to spice." Tabbouleh is common all over the Middle East, with regional variations in Lebanon and Syria. The Lebanese tend to prefer a greener (that is, more parsley-heavy) version; Syrian tradition bulks it up with more bulgur.

cook's note
When the flavor counts (and it always counts), freshly squeezed lemon juice is the way to go.

sesame tofu stir-fry serves 2 to 4 • prep time: 45 minutes (half inactive)

1	block firm tofu (14 to 15 ounces)	2	teaspoons sugar	8	ounces snow peas
¼	cup soy sauce	2	teaspoons sesame seeds	3	tablespoons vegetable oil
1	tablespoon dark sesame oil	1	1-inch piece fresh ginger	2	tablespoons water
1	tablespoon rice vinegar	2	scallions	2	to 4 cups cooked white or brown rice, for serving
		1	clove garlic		

1. Drain the tofu and cut into 1-inch cubes (about 24 pieces). Whisk soy sauce, sesame oil, vinegar, and sugar in a glass pie plate or baking dish. Add tofu, turn to coat, and set aside for 30 minutes.

2. Meanwhile, toast the sesame seeds in a small dry skillet over medium heat, stirring and tossing, until fragrant and a shade or two darker, about 4 minutes. Pour into a bowl to cool. Peel and grate the ginger. Trim and chop the scallions, keeping the white and green parts separate. Smash, peel, and finely chop the garlic. Pull off the stems and any tough strings from the snow peas, if necessary.

▶ know-how 99

3. When you're ready to cook the tofu, reserve 1 tablespoon of the marinade in a small bowl and drain off the rest. Pat the tofu dry with paper towels. Heat 2 tablespoons oil in a large nonstick skillet or wok over medium-high to high heat. Working in batches if necessary, fry the tofu in the skillet, turning occasionally, until golden, about 7 minutes. Transfer the tofu with a slotted spoon or spatula; toss with the sesame seeds. Set aside.

4. Add the remaining oil to the skillet. Stir-fry the ginger, garlic, and scallion whites until fragrant, about 30 seconds. Add the snow peas and water and stir-fry until the snow peas are bright green and

lightly glazed, about 2 minutes. Return the fried tofu and scallion greens to the pan, pour in reserved marinade, and stir gently to combine. Cook until the snow peas are crisp-tender, about 2 minutes more. Serve with rice.

TIPS shopsmart
Snow peas are sweet and crisp—buy vibrantly colored ones with no spots or discoloring. Usually their "strings" are removed before they're sold, but if you see prominent strings sticking out of one end when you get them home, snap back the stem end and pull off the string. See tips for buying tofu, page 190, and stir-fry tips on page 140.

vegetables

You already know they're good for you. But did you know they're delicious?

vegetable wisdom
There's lots of vegetable variety out there—whether you're feeling like dark green and leafy or bright orange and sweet.

shop
- Vegetables have seasons. It's intuitive; think about what you want to eat when. Lighter in summer (corn, zucchini, tomatoes); more filling in winter (potatoes, cauliflower, squash). Check out farmers' markets for seasonal inspiration. In general, you want perky, appealing-looking vegetables without too many brown spots. And there's nothing wrong with frozen vegetables (corn, peas, spinach, pearl onions, or lima beans) in a pinch.

prep
- All veggies should be rinsed before cooking. For peeling, seeding, and chopping, follow chart directions (pages 207-209), keeping in mind that same(ish)-size pieces will cook evenly.

cook
- The easiest ways to cook vegetables are roasting, boiling, and steaming. Roasting brings out the nutty, sweet flavors in vegetables; boiling and steaming intensify what's already there.

to roast vegetables
- Preheat oven to 425°F. Put vegetables, cut sides down, in a single layer in the pan and roast according to times and cues on pages 207-209, stirring half way through cooking time.

to boil green vegetables
- Bring a pot of water to a boil and add lots of salt, then add the veggies and cook, uncovered, draining in a colander when done (crisp-tender or a little softer to bring out the flavor).

to boil root vegetables (like potatoes and carrots)
- Salt a pot of cold water, add the vegetables, and bring to a boil. Cook until done (if you can pierce them with a fork and they fall off). Drain in a colander.

to steam all vegetables
- Pour about an inch of water into a skillet or wok and bring to a boil over medium-high heat. Put vegetables into a steamer basket (line the basket with sliced lemons or herbs, if you want) and season with salt. Set the steamer over the boiling water, cover, and cook to crisp-tender.
- When they're done, toss them with anything from olive oil and lemon to hoisin sauce and sesame seeds, or salsa, tapenade, hot sauce, salad dressing, mustard, chutney, or soy sauce—check out the charts on the following pages for ideas.

roasting vegetables

vegetable	prep	how to roast	finish with
asparagus	hold both ends of stalk and bend until it snaps	**toss lightly:** OO/S/P **roast:** 10 to 14 minutes **cue:** tips brown	a sprinkle of freshly grated Parmesan
beets	cut off leafy tops (leaving about ½ inch of stem); don't peel	**toss:** OO/S/P sprinkle w/water and herbs (optional); wrap in foil **roast:** 40 to 50 minutes **cue:** pierce with paring knife; should fall off knife easily	toss with fresh rosemary and orange zest
broccoli	cut into florets see page 101	**toss:** OO/S/P **roast:** 14 to 16 minutes **cue:** browned and nutty tasting	toss with toasted nuts
brussels sprouts	pull off loose or discolored leaves; trim stems flush with bottom of sprouts	**toss:** OO/S/P **roast:** 15 to 20 minutes **cue:** browned, nutty	a squeeze of lemon
carrots	peel; leave whole	**toss:** OO/S/P **roast:** 12 to 15 minutes or seal in foil and roast 20 minutes **cue:** tender and sweet	toss with mustard or grated fresh ginger
cauliflower	cut into florets see page 101	**toss:** OO/S/P or MB/S/P **roast:** 15 minutes **cue:** browned, sweet, nutty	toss with tapenade
corn	peel back husks and remove silk; to boil: husk fully	**drizzle:** with OO/S/P; put husks back in place **roast on oven rack:** 15 to 20 minutes **cue:** husks golden brown; corn tender	salsa or chili powder
eggplant (italian or japanese)	cut into 1½-inch chunks (don't peel)	**toss:** OO/S/P **roast:** (leave lots of space between pieces) 25 to 30 minutes **cue:** tender, firm, rich brown	minced garlic and lemon juice; pesto or soy sauce; fennel seeds
fennel	quarter or slice see page 101	**toss:** OO/S/P **roast:** 20 minutes **cue:** sweet and golden brown	fresh herbs or Parmesan

OO = olive oil   S = salt
MB = melted butter   P = pepper

vegetable	prep	how to roast	finish with
garlic	cut about ½ inch off the pointy end of the head to expose cloves	**drizzle:** OO/S/P wrap in foil **roast:** 30 minutes **cue:** cloves are soft, slip easily from their skins	great by itself, or smeared on bread or corn
red or yellow onions	peel and cut into quarters or sixths through the root; leave root end intact	**drizzle:** OO/S **roast:** 30 to 40 minutes **cue:** knife goes through center, edges charred and crisp	toss with balsamic vinegar
parsnips	peel. leave whole if small; if large, cut into even-size chunks; trim tough woody core if old	**drizzle:** OO/S **roast:** 16 to 20 minutes **cue:** browned and tender	sprinkle with minced parsley
portobello mushrooms	remove stem; trim dark gills (optional)	**brush cap:** OO/S **roast:** 10 minutes, cap side down. pour off juice, turn cap up, sprinkle with S, and roast 10 more minutes **cue:** cap soft, edges crispy and brown	toss with vinegar or fresh herbs
button or shiitake mushrooms	remove stem	**toss:** OO/S/P **roast:** 15 to 25 minutes, depending on size **cue:** cap soft; edges crispy and brown	toss with soy sauce and freshly grated ginger
potatoes	see recipes, pages 212–216	see recipes pages 212 and 215	what isn't good on a potato? herbs, garlic, miso, tapenade, salsa, etc.
scallions	trim white roots and ragged green ends; peel off tough outer layers see page 99	**drizzle:** OO/S **roast:** 6 to 10 minutes **cue:** browned, tender	great by itself
shallots	leave whole; don't peel	**toss:** OO/S/P **roast:** 20 to 25 minutes **cue:** browned, tender	great by itself
sweet potatoes	wash well; cut lengthwise into wedges or poke with a fork to roast whole	**toss** (for wedges; rub over whole): OO/S **roast:** 40 to 45 minutes whole, 25 minutes wedges **cue:** browned and tender	dot with aioli (page 163) or drizzle with OO
tomatoes	halve crosswise; squeeze out the seeds (optional)	**drizzle:** OO/S/P **roast:** cut side up, 20 minutes **cue:** soft, juicy	fresh soft herbs (see page 103 for a guide) and minced garlic

OO = olive oil   **S** = salt
MB = melted butter   **P** = pepper

vegetable	prep	how to roast	finish with
turnips/rutabagas	peel and cut into quarters (if small) or 1½-inch chunks	**drizzle:** OO or MB/S/P **roast:** 25 to 30 minutes **cue:** browned and tender	MB and pinch brown sugar
winter squash	halve; remove seeds; cut into wedges or slices if desired (see page 102)	**drizzle:** OO or MB/S/P **roast:** 40 to 60 minutes, depending on size **cue:** fork tender; sweet; browned	freshly grated Parmesan, herbs like sage or rosemary, hot sauce
zucchini/yellow squash	cut crosswise into ½-inch-thick slices	**roast:** 10 to 13 minutes **cue:** wrinkled skin, tender, sweet	pesto

steaming and boiling vegetables

vegetable	steaming/boiling	finish with
asparagus	**steam:** 4 to 6 minutes, depending on thickness	MB or OO and a squeeze of lemon
beets	**boil:** 20 to 30 minutes	vinegar and OO
broccoli	**steam:** 4 to 6 minutes for crisp, 8 to 10 for tender **boil:** 2 to 3 minutes	red pepper flakes and minced garlic
brussels sprouts	**boil or steam:** 8 to 10 minutes	orange zest or crumbled cooked bacon
carrots	**boil or steam:** 4 to 6 minutes	MB and dill (or other mild herbs)
cauliflower	**boil or steam:** 4 to 8 minutes	lemon zest or browned butter (see page 185)
corn	**boil:** 3 to 6 minutes, depending on size of kernels	MB or olive oil, paprika
fennel	**steam:** 10 minutes	OO and orange or lemon zest
potatoes	boil or steam until fork-tender, 10 to 45 minutes	MB, herbs, OO, or salsa
scallions	**steam:** 3 minutes	toasted sesame oil and grated ginger
turnips/rutabagas	**boil or steam:** 8 minutes	MB and parsley

green beans with shallots serves 4 • prep time: 20 minutes

½ teaspoon kosher salt, plus more
 for the cooking water
1 pound fresh green beans
1 large shallot
1 to 2 tablespoons extra-virgin
 olive oil
 Freshly ground black pepper

1. Bring a medium pot of water to a boil over high heat and salt it generously. Trim the stem ends off the green beans. Peel and finely chop the shallot.

2. Drop the green beans into the boiling water and cook, uncovered, until crisp-tender, about 4 minutes. Drain in a colander and rinse with very cold water until cool. Drain well and pat dry with paper towels. (The vegetables can be prepared up to this point up to 4 hours ahead.)

3. Heat the olive oil in a large skillet over medium heat. Add the shallot and cook, stirring occasionally, until the shallot is just golden, about 2 minutes. Add the green beans, increase the heat to high, and cook, stirring occasionally, until the beans are heated through, about 4 minutes. Season with the ½ teaspoon salt and some black pepper and serve immediately.

shopsmart
TIPS Look for smooth, crisp green beans with velvety skin. If they're pretrimmed, make sure the trimmed end is moist-looking. See note on shallots, page 165.

wilted spinach serves 4 • prep time: 15 minutes

2 pounds spinach (about
 2 big bunches)
1 large clove garlic
2 to 3 tablespoons extra-virgin
 olive oil
 Kosher salt and freshly ground
 black pepper
4 lemon wedges (optional)

1. Remove and discard spinach stems. Tear leaves into large pieces. Fill a large bowl with cold water and wash the spinach, lifting it out of the water to leave the dirt and grit in the bowl. Repeat with fresh water 2 or 3 times or until the spinach is clean. Drain in a colander.

2. Smash and peel the garlic. In a large skillet over medium heat add half the oil. Add the garlic and stir until it begins to turn golden,

about 3 minutes. Remove the garlic and discard. Add the spinach in batches, stirring with tongs to wilt before adding more. When all the spinach has been added, raise the heat to high, season with salt and black pepper, and cook, covered, for 3 minutes. Drain the spinach in a colander or remove with tongs, taking care to shake excess water into the pan. Serve in a medium bowl, drizzled with the remaining oil and garnished with lemon wedges, if desired.

▶ know-how 99

shopsmart
TIPS Two pounds of spinach might seem like a lot for 4 people, but a mountain of spinach wilts down almost totally once cooked. Always go with more than you think you need when you're cooking leafy greens.

crispy broccoli with spicy garlic serves 4 • prep time: 20 minutes

½   teaspoon kosher salt, plus more
     for cooking water
1   bunch broccoli
4   cloves garlic
3   tablespoons extra-virgin
     olive oil
     Pinch crushed red pepper flakes

1. Bring a medium pot of water to a boil over high heat and salt it generously. Cut broccoli tops into small florets. Peel any tough or woody skin from the remaining stalks and thinly slice crosswise. Smash, peel and thinly slice garlic.

▶ know-how 101, 99

2. Drop the broccoli into the boiling water and cook, uncovered, until crisp-tender, about 3 minutes. Drain in a colander and rinse with very cold water until cool. Drain well and pat as dry as you can with paper towels. (The vegetables can be prepared up to this point, up to 4 hours ahead.)

3. Put the garlic and olive oil in a large skillet and heat over medium-high heat. Cook, swirling the pan so the garlic cooks evenly, until it is just golden, about 5 minutes. Remove garlic with a slotted spoon or pick out with tongs, leaving the olive oil behind. Set garlic aside.

4. Put broccoli florets in the pan and scatter the cut stalks on top. Sprinkle with the red pepper flakes. Cook over medium-high heat, without stirring, for about 1 minute to dry up some of the water the broccoli releases. Continue cooking, shaking pan occasionally to move broccoli around, until crispy at the edges, about 5 minutes. Return garlic to the pan and toss to combine. Season with the ½ teaspoon salt and serve immediately.

TIPS

shopsmart
A stalk of broccoli is one tree-shape piece; a bunch is a cluster of stalks. Buy thin-stemmed, tightly closed bunches with even, green color.

cook's note
Don't stir the broccoli; instead, shake the pan so the pieces move but don't break.

sautéed mushrooms serves 2 to 4 • prep time: 15 minutes

10 ounces button or cremini
     mushrooms
     Handful fresh flat-leaf parsley
     leaves (optional)
2   to 3 tablespoons unsalted butter
     Kosher salt and freshly ground
     black pepper

1. Brush the mushrooms if they are dirty but don't wash them. Trim any tough stems, if necessary, and quarter the mushrooms. Chop the parsley, if using.

▶ know-how 103

2. Heat a large skillet over high heat. Add about half the butter. Once it melts, add the mushrooms and cook, without stirring or moving them, until they brown, about 4 minutes. Toss or stir the mushrooms. Cook until nicely browned all over, 2 to 3 minutes more, adding more butter as the mushrooms absorb it. Season with salt and black pepper to taste. Toss with the parsley, if using, and serve.

TIPS

cook's note
See note on mushrooms, page 85.

roasted potatoes with garlic & parsley
serves 4 • prep time: 40 to 50 minutes

1½ pounds small or medium
   red potatoes
2 tablespoons extra-virgin
   olive oil
1 teaspoon kosher salt, plus more
   for seasoning
2 to 3 cloves garlic
   Small handful fresh flat-leaf
   parsley leaves
   Freshly ground black pepper

1. Preheat oven to 375°F. Scrub the spuds, leaving the skin on. Halve the potatoes if small; quarter if medium. Toss the potatoes in a medium bowl with the olive oil and 1 teaspoon salt. Spread the potatoes, arranging them in a single layer, cut sides down, in a roasting pan. Roast until golden brown, 30 to 40 minutes.

2. Meanwhile, smash and peel the garlic. Finely chop the garlic and parsley together. Remove the roasting pan from the oven; add the garlic mixture to the potatoes, and stir to coat (a metal spatula is ideal for this). Continue to roast until the potatoes and garlic are evenly browned, about 5 minutes more. (Take care that the garlic doesn't burn.) Season with salt and black pepper to taste.

▶ know-how 99, 103

make it your own
Add extra herbs, like thyme and rosemary, or cook the potatoes in bacon drippings, or toss with your favorite spice blend, like chili powder, herbes de Provence, or curry powder.

shopsmart
TIPS Potatoes can be divided into two categories: waxy and floury (or boiling potatoes and baking potatoes). Waxy potatoes, like all the ones below, are lower in starch, hold their shape well, and are generally better boiled, steamed, or roasted, or used in potato salad. Floury potatoes, like the russet potato on the opposite page, are starchier and tend to be fluffier when mashed or baked.

red

blue

yukon gold

mashed potatoes serves 4 • prep time: 50 minutes

- 2 pounds russet potatoes (about 4 medium)
- 1½ teaspoons kosher salt, plus more for cooking the potatoes
- 4 to 8 tablespoons unsalted butter
- ¾ to 1 cup whole milk
  Freshly ground black pepper

1. Lightly scrub the potatoes. Put them in a large saucepan with cold water to cover by about 3 inches and season generously with salt. Bring to a boil over high heat. Lower the heat to maintain a gentle simmer and cook until the potatoes are fork-tender, 40 to 45 minutes.

2. Drain the potatoes in a colander. Let the potatoes cool just until you can handle them—hot potatoes mash better. Meanwhile, melt the butter in a small saucepan over low heat.

3. Hold the potatoes in a towel or oven mitt and gently peel the skins off with a knife or your fingers. Quarter the potatoes and put them back in the pan.

4. Heat the milk in a microwave-safe measuring cup or bowl until

hot. Add the butter to the potatoes and mash with a fork or potato masher until most of the lumps are gone and the potatoes are smooth and fluffy. Then stir in the milk until the mashed potatoes are light and smooth. If there are still lumps, paddle them smooth with a wooden spoon. Season with 1½ teaspoons salt, or to taste, and black pepper to taste. Serve immediately.

mashed potato wisdom
Cooking unpeeled potatoes gives you the best-possible texture and flavor—and it's the easiest way. Mashing just-cooked hot potatoes keeps the texture light and not too starchy. For super-creamy potatoes, you'll probably want to use a food mill or a potato ricer, but for basic mash, all you really need is a fork and some biceps. Never use a food processor; they'll get gluey.

upgrades
Add fresh herbs, grated cheese, horseradish, chiles, or crisp-cooked and crumbled bacon.

one potato, two potato

Got a baked potato and an imagination? Then you've got the makings for all kinds of variations on sides or mains, as well as killer leftovers.

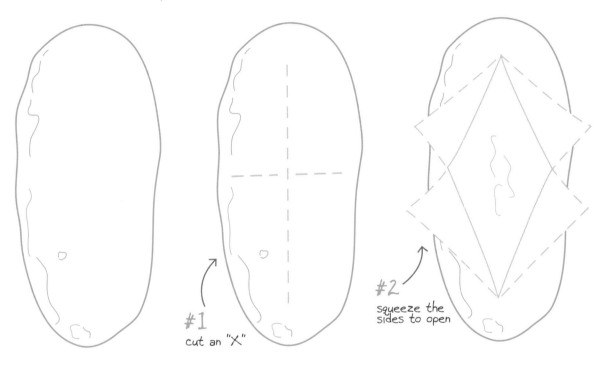

#1
cut an "X"

#2
squeeze the sides to open

make it:
american
quick beef chili (page 161) and cheese

italian
extra-virgin olive oil and freshly grated parmesan

asian
sriracha-miso dressing (page 91)

mexican
fresh tomato salsa (page 40, or store-bought) and shredded cheddar or your favorite Mexican cheese

take a baked potato and top it, stuff it, or fry it

baked potato
serves 4 • prep time: 1 hour

4   russet potatoes
     (about 8 ounces each)
     Vegetable oil (optional)

serving suggestions:
butter, sour cream, thinly
sliced chives or scallions, kosher
salt, freshly ground black pepper

1. Position an oven rack in the
center of the oven and preheat
oven to 425°F.

2. Scrub each potato and dry
well. For extra-crispy potato skins,
rub the outside of the potatoes
with vegetable oil. (Definitely
do this if you're making stuffed
potatoes.) Set the potatoes spaced
evenly directly on the oven rack.

3. Bake for 30 minutes. Then,
using an oven mitt to hold the
hot potatoes, prick each one with
a fork 3 or 4 times. Turn potatoes
and bake until potato is cooked
through, about 30 minutes more.
To test for doneness, squeeze
each potato with your thumb and
forefinger. If the skin remains
compressed, the potato is cooked
through. Slice open and serve with
the topping of your choice.

stuffed potato with broccoli & cheese
serves 4 • prep time: 1 hour
10 minutes

4   baked potatoes, still warm
1   small bunch broccoli
4   tablespoons (½ stick)
     unsalted butter
1   teaspoon kosher salt
     Freshly ground black pepper
4   to 6 ounces shredded sharp
     cheddar cheese

1. While the potatoes bake,
separate broccoli into florets and
trim and slice the tender part of the
stems. Place broccoli in a steamer
insert over simmering water, cover
and steam 8 to 10 minutes or until
tender. Chop into small pieces.

▶ know-how 101

2. Preheat broiler. Take each
warm cooked potato, slice a
lengthwise slit in the top, and
gently scoop out some of the flesh,
leaving enough to give the potato
skin structure. Mix the potato
flesh, butter, salt, and some black
pepper in a bowl with fork, then
gently stir in broccoli pieces. Refill
each potato with the mixture.
Sprinkle a heaping handful of
cheese over the top of each potato.
Set on a rimmed baking sheet and
run under the broiler until the
cheese melts and gets golden brown
and bubbly in spots, about
5 minutes.

variation
Use cooked cauliflower and good-
quality aged Gouda cheese.

homestyle hash browns
serves 4 • prep time: 25 minutes

4   leftover baked potatoes
1   medium onion
6   tablespoons unsalted butter
     Kosher salt and freshly ground
     black pepper

1. Roughly dice the baked
potatoes, skins and all. Peel and
chop the onion.

▶ know-how 99

2. Melt the butter in a large
skillet over medium-high heat.
When butter is hot, add onions and
cook, stirring occasionally, until
soft, about 5 minutes. Add the
potatoes, season with salt and
pepper, and cook, stirring only
occasionally, until some potatoes
get crisp and brown while others
remain tender. The potatoes may
stick to the bottom; let them get
crispy and brown, then scrape
them off and stir the crunchy
bits back into the hash. Keep this
up until the potatoes are mostly
browned and the onions are soft,
about 15 minutes. Serve hot.

picnic potato salad serves 4 to 6 • prep time: 20 minutes

½ medium red onion
2 pounds small red-skinned waxy potatoes (about 10 to 12 potatoes)
2 tablespoons plus 1 teaspoon kosher salt
2 ribs celery, with leaves
Small handful fresh flat-leaf parsley leaves
½ cup mayonnaise
2 tablespoons sweet pickle relish
1 tablespoon mustard (whole-grain, Dijon, or yellow)
Freshly ground black pepper

1. Chop the red onion and soak in a bowl of cold water while you prep the rest of the salad.
▶ know-how 99

2. Scrub the potatoes, leaving the skin on. Halve the potatoes if small, quarter if medium, and put in a medium saucepan with cold water to cover by about 2 inches; add 2 tablespoons kosher salt. Bring to a boil, lower the heat, and simmer until fork tender, 8 to 10 minutes. Drain in a colander in the sink. (If the potatoes are very tender, rinse briefly with cool water.) Set aside to cool. Thinly slice the celery and

chop the leaves. Drain onions and pat dry. Add onions and celery to the potatoes.
▶ know-how 100

3. Chop the parsley. Whisk the mayonnaise, relish, mustard, parsley, and remaining salt and black pepper to taste together in a large bowl. When the potatoes are cool, fold them into the mayonnaise mixture until evenly dressed. Take care not to overwork the salad or the potatoes will get mushy. Serve immediately or refrigerate until ready to serve.
▶ know-how 103

upgrades
• Add 2 hard-boiled eggs, roughly chopped.
• Use dill with or instead of parsley.
• Scatter crumbled bacon on top.

cook's note
TIPS If you're packing this up to take on the go, make sure it's cold—keep it in a cooler with some insulated ice packs. Discard any leftovers that spend too long out of the fridge. (See page 13 for more food safety info.)

marinated roasted peppers serves 4 • prep time: 1 hour 20 minutes

3   red, yellow, or orange bell
    peppers (or a combination)
¼   to ⅓ cup extra-virgin olive oil
1   tablespoon vinegar (white wine,
    red wine, or balsamic)
    Fresh thyme, oregano, or
    rosemary sprigs (optional)
1   teaspoon kosher salt
    Freshly ground black pepper

1. Position an oven rack in the upper part of the oven and preheat the broiler. Line a broiler pan (or baking sheet) with foil. Halve the peppers through the stem and remove the seeds and stems. Lay the peppers, cut sides down, on the prepared baking sheet. Broil the peppers, moving as needed, until the skins char evenly, 8 to 10 minutes. Put the broiled peppers in a large bowl, cover with a plate, pot lid, or plastic wrap, and set aside until just cool enough to handle, about 5 minutes. (Don't leave them sitting there for too long or they'll get muddy looking from the charred skins.)

▶ know-how 101

2. Rub skins off peppers with your fingers or a knife and lightly rinse with cool water, if necessary, to remove any remaining skin. Slice the peppers into strips about ¾ inch thick. Toss them in a bowl with the olive oil, vinegar, and herb sprigs, if using. Season with the salt and some black pepper to taste. Set aside at room temperature for 1 hour before serving to let the flavors come together. Store, covered, in the refrigerator for up to a week.

roasting

peeling

TIPS

shopsmart
Get thick-flesh, smooth-skinned peppers with fat stems. Pick up a couple and take the heaviest ones. We're not big fans of regular green peppers, but if you need some green, poblano peppers taste great cooked this way.

cook's note
These are incredibly versatile and good to have around. They're tasty in sandwiches, on pizza, or in omelettes or diced into risotto.

eggplant parmesan
serves 4 to 6 • prep time: 1 hour 40 minutes

1 eggplant (about 1 pound)
  Kosher salt
  All-purpose flour
3 large eggs
1 cup plain dry bread crumbs
1 teaspoon dried oregano
½ cup plus 2 tablespoons
  extra-virgin olive oil
1 28-ounce can whole peeled
  tomatoes
2 cloves garlic
1½ teaspoons kosher salt
1 large handful fresh basil leaves
1 ball fresh salted mozzarella
  (about ½ pound)
½ cup freshly grated Parmesan
  cheese

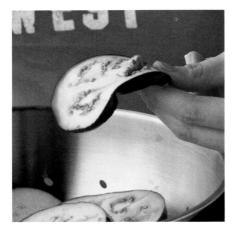

1. Trim the ends from the eggplant, but don't peel it. Slice into rounds no more than ½ inch thick—the thinner, the better. Season both sides generously with salt and place in a colander set in the sink to drain for about 1 hour. Rinse salt off slices and pat them very dry.

2. Preheat the oven to 375°F. Place about a cup of flour on a plate or shallow bowl. Beat the eggs in another bowl and combine the bread crumbs and oregano in a third. Dip each eggplant slice in the flour, shake off the excess, then dip into the eggs, and press both sides into the bread crumbs to coat.

3. Heat ½ cup olive oil in a large skillet over medium-high heat. Fry the eggplant in batches until crisp and deep golden brown, turning halfway through cooking, about 4 minutes total. Set aside on paper towels to drain.

4. Pour the oil out of the skillet and wipe clean with a paper towel. Pour the tomatoes and their juices in a large bowl and crush with your hands. Smash and peel the garlic. Return the skillet to medium heat and add remaining 2 tablespoons oil. Add the garlic and cook until lightly golden, about 1 minute. Carefully pour the tomatoes into the skillet and season with the 1½ teaspoons salt. Simmer until the sauce just thickens, about 8 to 10 minutes. Add the basil and cook until just wilted, about 1 to 2 minutes.

▶ know-how 99

5. Lay the eggplant in slightly overlapping rows in a medium casserole. Pour about ⅔ of the sauce over the eggplant. Thinly slice the mozzarella and layer over the sauce. Cover with the rest of the sauce and scatter the Parmesan on top. Bake, uncovered, until the sauce is bubbly and the cheeses melt, about 20 minutes. Let "settle" for 5 minutes before serving.

know-how 99

shopsmart
TIPS
• Look for solid colored, smooth-skinned, firm eggplant with no soft spots or spongy parts. Italian eggplant are somewhat smaller and thinner than American eggplant, but taste essentially the same; Japanese eggplant are smaller still, with thin skin and a slightly sweet taste.
• See page 56 for how to buy and store fresh mozzarella.

provencal vegetable gratin serves 4 to 6 • prep time: 1 hour 10 minutes

2   medium onions
3   cloves garlic
3   to 4 sprigs fresh thyme
4   tablespoons extra-virgin olive oil
2   teaspoons kosher salt
3   ripe medium plum tomatoes
3   medium zucchini, yellow, or other summer squash (or a combination)
   Freshly ground black pepper
⅓   cup finely grated grana-style cheese, such as Parmesan

1. Preheat the oven to 375°F. Peel and slice the onion. Smash and peel the garlic. Strip the thyme leaves from the stems.

▶ know-how 99, 103

2. Heat 2 tablespoons of the olive oil in a large skillet over medium heat. Add the onions, garlic, 1 teaspoon of the salt, and the thyme. Cover and cook, stirring occasionally, until the onions are wilted, about 5 minutes; uncover and cook over high heat until most of the excess moisture evaporates (but don't let the onions brown), about 10 minutes. Spread cooked onions on the bottom of an 8x11-inch baking dish.

3. While the onions cook, thinly slice the tomatoes and zucchini crosswise (ideally about ⅓ inch thick). Toss sliced vegetables in a large bowl with remaining 2 tablespoons olive oil, 1 teaspoon salt, and some black pepper. Scatter the vegetables over the onions, spreading them out in an even layer. Scatter the cheese evenly over the vegetables. Cover the dish with aluminum foil and bake until the vegetables get juicy, 30 to 40 minutes. Uncover and cook until cheese begins to brown, 20 to 30 minutes more. Serve hot or at room temperature.

▶ know-how 105

make it your own
Many different herbs work here; if you've got basil, use that, or even fresh marjoram, if it's available. Dress it up by arranging the vegetables in patterns or strips, or by adding some thinly sliced eggplant for another layer of color.

 a side of history
The word "gratin" comes from the 16th-century French for "to scrape" and originally referred to the cooked-on crust certain dishes left on pots and pans. In the 19th century the meaning changed to refer to any dish with a deliberately browned crust on top.

maple-roasted butternut squash serves 4 • prep time: 45 minutes

1 butternut squash, about
   2½ pounds

¼ cup real maple syrup
1 tablespoon unsalted butter

1 teaspoon chipotle hot sauce
1 teaspoon kosher salt

1. Preheat the oven to 425°F. Cut the stem off the squash. Halve the squash lengthwise, then halve again lengthwise to make quarters. Scoop out the seeds with a spoon. Lay the quarters, cut sides up, on a foil-lined baking sheet.

▶ know-how 102

2. Combine the maple syrup and butter in a microwave-safe bowl or measuring cup. Cover with plastic wrap. Microwave on HIGH until

the butter melts. Carefully remove the plastic wrap and stir in the hot sauce and salt.

3. Pour half the sauce over the squash, making sure it pools in the seed cavity. Roast for 10 minutes. Remove from the oven, turn the squash to coat it in the sauce, and arrange the pieces with cut sides down. Return to the oven and cook until the sides in contact with the pan begin to caramelize,

10 to 15 minutes. Turn the other cut side down and continue to cook until browned and tender, about 15 minutes more. Transfer wedges to a platter and drizzle with the remaining sauce.

make it your own

Add fresh sage, rosemary, or thyme to the butter instead of hot sauce or try another variety of winter squash, like acorn, delicata, or sweet dumpling.

shopsmart
TIPS Buy the hardest squash you can find, with fat, full stems and nonshiny skin.

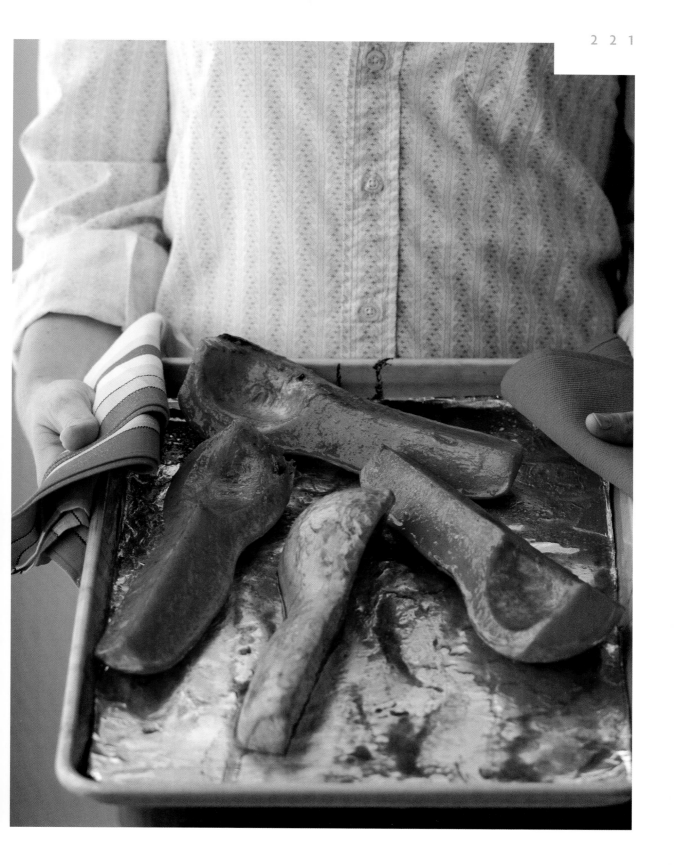

dessert

Homemade desserts say comfort and care like nothing else. And besides, they taste fabulous.

baking wisdom

Successful baking is in the details. Here's how to get them right.

ingredient rules
- There's a reason certain ingredients need to be certain temperatures: Room-temperature eggs beat up fluffier; cream whips best ice-cold; and, though cold butter makes the flakiest pie crust, room-temp butter makes the lightest cakes.
- Sugars (powdered, white, light brown, and dark brown) all come from the same plant. White sugar adds both flavor and texture to baked goods. Brown sugar is a combination of sugar and naturally occurring molasses; whether it's light or dark brown depends on how much molasses. To keep brown sugars moist, transfer the plastic bag from the box to a tightly sealed container. Powdery confectioners' sugar—a blend of sugar and a little corn starch—is good for sweetening whipped cream or decorating baked goods.
- Most baking recipes call for all-purpose flour. Cake flour (which we prefer for our birthday cake on page 241) gives certain baked goods a lighter, softer texture. Look for it near the all-purpose flour.
- Baking soda and powder last about 6 months after being opened. If you're not sure if they're still good, mix a pinch of your soda or powder with vinegar or hot water, respectively. If they fizz, you're in business.

method rules
- You won't find any difficult techniques in these recipes, but the right technique—like whisking dry ingredients so they're evenly mixed, or using a light touch with chocolate chip cookies—does make a difference. If you really get into baking, you'll want to get a handle on what various terms (like folding, whisking, and creaming) mean. Check out our website (foodnetwork.com) for detailed video directions.

oven rules
- Preheating the oven is key for good color and texture. It takes 20 minutes for an oven to hit its stride; turn it on early.
- Ovens differ; every oven has hot spots. Rotate your pans around once during baking to make sure everything cooks evenly—except when you're baking cakes. Opening the oven door too often can make a cake fall.

deep-dish brownies

makes about 24 (1½-inch) squares or 16 (2-inch) squares • prep time: 50 minutes plus cooling time

½ cup (1 stick) unsalted butter, plus more for the baking dish

4 ounces unsweetened chocolate
1 cup packed light brown sugar
¾ cup white sugar
½ teaspoon fine salt

1½ teaspoons pure vanilla extract
4 large cold eggs
1 cup all-purpose flour

1. Position a rack in the lower third of the oven and heat oven to 325°F. Line an 8x8-inch square metal or glass baking pan with foil so it hangs over the edges by about an inch. Butter the bottom and sides of the foil-lined pan.

2. In a microwave-safe bowl, melt chocolate and butter in the microwave on 75% power for 2 minutes. Stir, and microwave until both are completely melted, about 2 minutes more. (Or put the chocolate and butter in a heatproof bowl. Bring a saucepan filled with an inch or so of water to a very slow simmer; set the bowl on the pan without letting it touch the water. Stir occasionally until mixture is melted and smooth.)

3. Stir the sugars, salt, and vanilla into the chocolate mixture with a wooden spoon. Add the eggs and beat vigorously until fully incorporated. The batter should be thick and glossy. Add the flour and stir gently just until it disappears into the chocolate.

▶ know-how 107, 108

4. Pour batter into the prepared pan and bake until the top is crispy and a toothpick inserted into the middle comes out mostly clean, with a few crumbs, 40 to 50 minutes. (Go for the shorter time if you like your brownies on the gooey side.).

▶ know-how 108

5. Cool the brownies in the pan on the counter or on a rack if you have one. Lift the brownies out of the pan, using the foil as handles. Peel off the foil and cut brownies into squares.

make it your own
Add 1 cup chopped nuts just as the flour gets mixed in. Ice baked and cooled brownies with the Chocolate Glaze on page 234.

bowl-licking wisdom
A lot of people (like us) bake just for the bowl-licking privileges. Not to be a killjoy, but use caution if your dough's got raw eggs in it.

TIPS

shopsmart
We call for pure vanilla extract, which is made by steeping vanilla beans in alcohol. You'll get the richest, most vanilla-y flavor possible, short of whole beans (see page 108 for a primer on using whole beans).

cook's note
To butter foil (or a pan), take a chunk of butter in a bit of plastic wrap and run a thin coating all over the foil.

chocolate chip cookies makes 30 (2½-inch) cookies • prep time: 35 minutes

½   cup (1 stick) unsalted butter
¾   cup packed dark brown sugar
¾   cup white sugar
2   large eggs

1   teaspoon pure vanilla extract
2¼ cups all-purpose flour
¾   teaspoon baking soda
1   teaspoon fine salt

1   12-ounce bag semisweet
    chocolate chips or chunks, or
    half chips and half chopped
    nuts (about 2 cups)

1. Evenly position 2 racks in the middle of the oven and preheat oven to 375°F.

2. Put the butter in a microwave-safe bowl, cover, and microwave on medium power until melted. Or melt butter in a small saucepan. Cool slightly. Whisk the sugars, eggs, butter, and vanilla in a large bowl until smooth.
▶ know-how 108

3. Whisk the flour, baking soda, and salt in a small bowl. Stir

the dry ingredients into the wet ingredients with a wooden spoon, taking care not to overmix. Stir in the chocolate chips or chunks and nuts, if using.
▶ know-how 107

4. Line 2 baking sheets with parchment paper. Scoop heaping tablespoons of the dough onto the prepared baking sheets. Wet hands slightly and roll the dough into balls. Space the balls about 2 inches apart on the pans. Bake

until the cookies are golden but still soft in the center, 12 to 16 minutes, depending on how chewy or crunchy you like your cookies. Immediately transfer cookies with a spatula to a rack to cool.

storage wisdom
Put brownies or cookies in tightly sealed containers after they've cooled completely. Keep a piece of bread in the container if you're storing soft cookies; it keeps them moist and chewy.

TIPS

cook's note
• You can also freeze these to make ahead: Put the sheet with the raw balls of dough into the freezer for an hour. Then transfer the balls to plastic bags and freeze for up to 2 months, baking them straight from the freezer (in the oven or toaster oven) whenever you want them.
• If you only have one baking sheet, let it cool completely between batches.

fruit oatmeal crumble serves about 6 • prep time: 1 hour 10 minutes

crumble topping

- ½ cup all-purpose flour
- 1 cup quick-cooking oats
- ¾ cup packed light brown sugar
   Pinch fine salt
- 6 tablespoons unsalted butter
- ¾ cup chopped nuts, such as
   walnuts, almonds, or pecans

fruit

- 2 pounds baking pears, apples,
   or stone fruit such as peaches,
   apricots, or plums
- 2 to 4 tablespoons light brown or
   white sugar
- 2 tablespoons all-purpose flour
- ½ teaspoon pure vanilla extract
   Freshly grated nutmeg
   Pinch ground cinnamon
   Pinch fine salt

for serving:
ice cream or sweetened
   whipped cream

1. Preheat oven to 375°F.

2. For the crumble: Whisk the flour, oats, brown sugar, and salt in a medium bowl. Melt the butter, covered, in the microwave, or in a small saucepan on the stove. Add the melted butter to the flour mixture and toss together with a fork until evenly moistened; stir in the nuts. Squeeze handfuls of the crumble mixture together and drop them onto a cookie sheet to get a good proportion of large and small crumbs. Freeze for 10 minutes while you prepare the fruit.

▶ know-how 107

3. For the fruit: Halve, core, and slice the fruit and put in a large bowl. Toss the fruit with the sugar (use more or less depending on the sweetness of the fruit), flour, vanilla, nutmeg, cinnamon, and salt. Transfer to an 8x8-inch glass baking dish.

4. Evenly sprinkle the crumble mixture over the fruit and pack down lightly. Bake the crumble until the topping is golden brown and the fruit is juicy and bubbly, 40 to 45 minutes. Let sit for 5 to 10 minutes before serving. Serve warm with ice cream or whipped cream.

upgrade

Add ¼ cup dried cranberries to the sliced apples or pears.

salt wisdom

Why add salt to desserts? Salt intensifies the flavors that are already there; your dessert won't taste salty if you add salt—it'll just taste more like itself.

TIPS

shopsmart
Baking pears are firm fleshed and slightly less juicy than regular pears; you want them to hold their shape when they're cooked. Bosc pears and Anjou pears both work well for baking.

cook's note
This crumble topping keeps extremely well in the freezer. Make a double batch and keep half for the next time.

2-by-4 fruit salad serves 4 to 6 • prep time: 30 minutes

2   navel oranges or small
    grapefruits or 1 of each
2   cups berries, such as
    strawberries, raspberries,
    blackberries, blueberries,
    or a combination
2   bananas
2   pieces seasonal fruit (see
    Cook's Note, below)
¼   cup honey
¼   cup water or white wine
1   cinnamon stick
    Pinch kosher salt
½   vanilla bean
1   1-inch piece fresh ginger
    (optional)

1. Trim off all the peel and pith from the grapefruits and/or oranges, halve or quarter them top to bottom, and slice crosswise into thin pieces. Rinse the berries and pat dry on a paper towel. Halve or quarter the strawberries if large. Peel and slice the bananas. Prepare the seasonal fruit as needed. Toss all the fruit in a large bowl.

▶ know-how 104

2. Stir the honey, water, cinnamon stick, and salt together in a small saucepan. Split the vanilla bean lengthwise and use a paring knife to scrape the seeds out of the pod; add the seeds and pod to the pan. Thinly slice the ginger, if using, and add to pan. Bring to a boil and pour over the fruit. Set aside for 30 minutes to 1 hour for the flavors to come together. Remove ginger and vanilla bean (or tell people not to eat it) and serve.

▶ know-how 108, 99

upgrades:

Add a splash (2 tablespoons) of alcohol: Stir plain or flavored rum, brandy, or orange liqueur into the honey mixture after it comes off the heat and before you pour it over the fruit.

 cook's note
Two-by-four is a great rule for fruit salads in general: Think 2 each of 4 fruits. See page 20 for some guidelines on seasonal fruits, as well as shopping and storage. Try chunks of peaches, plums, or nectarines in summer; sliced apples or pears or a handful of grapes in fall; pomegranate seeds in winter; or quartered fresh figs in spring.

crepes serves 4 to 6 (12 crepes) • prep time: 1 hour

1	cup all-purpose flour	3	large eggs
2	tablespoons sugar	1	teaspoon pure vanilla extract
$\frac{1}{8}$	teaspoon fine salt	4	tablespoons unsalted butter
1	cup milk		About $\frac{3}{4}$ cup chocolate-hazelnut spread (such as Nutella)
$\frac{1}{4}$	cup water		

for serving:
ice cream or sweetened whipped cream

1. Whisk the flour, sugar, and salt together in a bowl or pulse in a food processor or blender. Gradually whisk in the milk, water, eggs, and vanilla extract or process or blend until smooth. Set aside for at least 30 minutes. (The batter can be made to this point a day ahead and refrigerated. Bring to room temperature before adding butter.)
▶ know-how 107, 108

2. Melt the butter in a small saucepan or in the microwave; whisk it into the batter. Pour the batter into a measuring cup with a pouring spout or a small pitcher. Have plates ready for serving.

3. Heat a medium nonstick skillet over medium heat until a drop of water bounces and sizzles in the pan before evaporating. Pour a little less than $\frac{1}{4}$ cup of crepe batter into the skillet and quickly swirl it to coat the pan evenly. Cook until the batter sets, about 1 to $1\frac{1}{2}$ minutes. The crepe will blister in the middle and the edges will get a little crispy. Using your fingers or a spatula, carefully pick the crepe up by its edges and flip it to cook the other side, 15 to 30 seconds. Repeat with remaining batter, serving or stacking the crepes as they cook.

4. To serve, spread about 1 tablespoon of the chocolate-hazelnut spread in the center of a warm crepe. Fold the top of the crepe over to make a half circle, then fold the right side over to make a triangle. Repeat with the remaining crepes. Serve 2 or 3 crepes per person, topped with a scoop of ice cream or a dollop of whipped cream.

make it your own

Peel and slice your favorite citrus fruit into small pieces. Sprinkle sugar on the warm crepe, then dot with the pieces of citrus.

crepe wisdom

Stack the crepes as they cook to keep them warm. Crepes can be made a day ahead, wrapped in plastic, and refrigerated. Bring to room temperature at least 1 hour before serving.

pour

swirl

4 things to do with a bar of chocolate

dip (when warm) and frost (when cold)

chocolate fondue or frosting

6 ounces bittersweet or semisweet chocolate

¼ cup heavy cream

drizzle over fruit, cake, or ice cream

chocolate sauce

6 ounces bittersweet or semisweet chocolate

6 tablespoons unsalted butter

¼ cup honey or corn syrup

stir into (hot or cold) milk

chocolate syrup

6 ounces bittersweet or semisweet chocolate

⅓ cup water

⅓ cup honey

glaze baked goods or make a chocolate shell for ice cream

chocolate glaze

6 ounces bittersweet or semisweet chocolate

8 tablespoons unsalted butter (1 stick)

1 tablespoon honey

1. Roughly chop the chocolate.

2. Put all the ingredients in a microwave-safe bowl or glass measuring cup. Microwave at 75% power until the chocolate melts, about 2 minutes. Remove from the microwave and whisk until fully combined, smooth, and glossy. Serve as desired.

ice cream wisdom

• Storebought ice cream should last for at least 2 months in the freezer; longer if stored correctly. Keep it frozen at all times; if it melts, refreezing it will make it icy and gummy.

• If you buy your ice cream in bulk, keep a layer of plastic wrap directly on its surface to help it stay creamy.

TIPS shopsmart
Bittersweet and semisweet chocolate are both milk-free and contain high percentages of unrefined chocolate. Semisweet chocolate is sweeter than bittersweet, but they're both less sweet than milk chocolate.

bread pudding with whiskey sauce
serves 4 • prep time: 1 hour 10 minutes

bread pudding
- 2 tablespoons unsalted butter, plus more for the baking dish
- ½ cup sugar, plus 1 tablespoon
- ¼ teaspoon ground cinnamon
- 3 large eggs
- 1 large egg yolk
- 2 cups half-and-half
- 2 tablespoons whiskey, bourbon, or rum
- 2 teaspoons pure vanilla extract
- ¼ teaspoon fine salt
  Pinch freshly grated nutmeg
- 10 slices white sandwich bread or 4 (1-inch-thick) slices challah

brown sugar whiskey sauce
- ½ cup packed dark brown sugar
- 2 tablespoons white sugar
- ½ cup heavy cream
  Pinch fine salt
- 1 to 2 tablespoons unsalted butter
- 2 to 3 tablespoons whiskey

1. Position an oven rack in the center of the oven and preheat oven to 325°F. Brush an 8x8-inch glass baking dish with some butter. Pour ½ cup sugar into the pan, turning to dust the bottom and sides with sugar. Pour the excess sugar into a large bowl. Stir the 1 tablespoon sugar and the cinnamon together in a small bowl.

▶ know-how 107

2. Whisk the eggs, egg yolk, half-and-half, whiskey, vanilla, salt, and nutmeg with the sugar in a large bowl. Cut the bread into approximately 1-inch cubes. Add about ¾ of the bread to the egg mixture and soak for 20 minutes.

3. Pour the bread mixture into the prepared baking dish. Scatter the remaining cup of bread cubes on top of the pudding and gently press them into the egg-soaked bread (if they don't get completely wet, don't worry about it).

4. Melt the 2 tablespoons butter in a small saucepan or in a bowl or cup covered with plastic wrap in the microwave, then brush the top of the bread pudding with butter. Sprinkle the cinnamon sugar on top and bake until golden brown on top and just set, 30 to 35 minutes. Serve with the Brown Sugar Whiskey Sauce.

brown sugar whiskey sauce
Put the sugars, cream, and salt in a medium saucepan. Bring to a boil, stirring until melted and smooth. Adjust the heat to maintain a simmer and cook, without stirring, until thicker, about 5 minutes. Pull the pan off the heat and whisk in the butter and whiskey to taste. Serve warm or at room temperature.

cook's note
TIPS Any whiskey is fine here; feel free to use bourbon, Tennessee whiskey, Irish whiskey, or Scotch, depending on your preference. (It's spelled "whiskey" if it's from Ireland or the U.S.A. and "whisky" from Canada or Scotland.) See page 121 for more notes on cooking with alcohol.

apple pie serves 6 to 8 • prep time: 2½ hours

dough
- 2½ cups all-purpose flour
- ¼ cup sugar
- ¾ teaspoon fine salt
- ½ cup (1 stick) unsalted butter, straight from the refrigerator
- ¼ cup shortening
- 1 large egg
- ¼ cup very cold water

filling
- 1 lemon
- 3 pounds baking apples, such as Golden Delicious, Cortland, or Mutsu (7 to 8 apples)
- ⅔ cup sugar, plus more for sprinkling on the pie
- ¼ teaspoon ground cinnamon
- Generous pinch freshly grated nutmeg
- ¼ teaspoon ground cardamom (optional)
- ¼ cup unsalted butter (½ stick)
- ½ teaspoon pure vanilla extract
- 2 to 3 tablespoons all-purpose flour
- 1 large egg

1. For the dough: Whisk the flour, sugar, and salt together in a medium bowl. Cut the butter into small cubes. Rub the shortening completely into the dry ingredients with your fingers. Then rub the cold butter into the mixture until it resembles cornmeal mixed with pea-size bits of butter. (If the mixture starts to get warm and sticky, refrigerate it to chill.) Beat the egg with the water, then drizzle it evenly over the dough. Lightly stir the dough together with a fork or by hand. The dough should just hold together when you squeeze it together, with some dry crumbly bits around the ball. If the dough is dry, sprinkle a little more cold water over the mixture. Alternatively, make dough in a food processor fitted with the metal blade. Pulse flour, sugar, and salt until combined. Cut butter into small cubes. Add shortening and butter and pulse about 10 times

until it resembles cornmeal mixed with bean-size bits of butter. Beat the egg and water together, add and pulse 1 to 2 times, but don't let the dough form into a ball in the machine. Remove the blade and bring the dough together by hand.

▶ know-how 107, 108

2. Divide the dough into 2 equal pieces. Wrap each piece in plastic wrap and shape each into a disk. Refrigerate at least 1 hour or up to 2 days.

3. For the filling: Finely grate lemon zest and squeeze juice into a large bowl. Peel apples, then cut the four "sides" off the apple, leaving the core behind. Cut each piece into 2 or 3 slices. Toss apples with lemon juice, ⅔ cup sugar, the cinnamon, nutmeg, and cardamom, if using.

▶ know-how 104

4. Melt the butter in a large skillet over medium-high heat. Add

TIPS

cook's note
• The dough can be refrigerated for up to 4 days or frozen for up to 2 months. Defrost frozen dough in the fridge overnight.
• The filling can be made up to 2 days ahead and refrigerated. Freeze the uncooked pie, if you want, but don't brush it with egg or dust it with sugar

beforehand. Place the pie in the freezer 30 minutes to harden it slightly and then double-wrap it with plastic wrap. Freeze for up to 6 months. When ready to bake, unwrap the pie, brush it with egg, and sprinkle with sugar. Bake from the frozen state until golden brown, about 1 hour and 10 minutes.

the apples and cook, stirring, until sugar dissolves and simmers, about 2 minutes. Cover, reduce heat to medium, and cook until the apples get soft and juicy, 10 to 15 minutes. Add the vanilla, sprinkle the flour over the fruit, and stir to mix evenly. Cool completely.

5. Lightly dust the counter with flour. Roll each dough disk into an 11- to 12-inch circle with a rolling pin. Layer the dough between waxed or parchment paper on a baking sheet and refrigerate for at least 10 minutes.

6. Beat the egg in a small bowl with a fork. Line a 9-inch glass pie pan with a dough circle, trimming so it hangs about ½ inch over the edge of the pan. Put the filling in the crust so it mounds slightly in the center. Brush the rim of the bottom crust with some of the egg. Place the second dough circle over the top and trim the overhang. Fold the top layer of dough under the edge of the bottom layer and press the edges together to form a seal. Flute the edge (see photo, right). Refrigerate the pie for at least 20 minutes. Meanwhile, place a rack in the lower third of the oven and preheat to 425°F.

7. Brush the top of the pie with beaten egg and sprinkle with sugar. Make several small slits in the top of the dough to allow steam to escape while baking. Put the pie on a baking sheet and bake for 15 minutes, then reduce the temperature to 375°F. Bake until the crust is golden brown, about 50 minutes more. Cool on a rack. Serve warm or at room temperature. Keep pie, covered, at room temperature for a day or refrigerate for up to 4 days.

shopsmart
• When we say baking apples, we mean the kind that won't turn into applesauce when cooked. Often you'll see apples sold as "baking apples" in the supermarket—of course, you can eat those raw too, but they're great in pie, since they hold their shape.
• See notes on cardamom, page 141.

pie wisdom
• Cold butter (and cold water) is key for perfect pie dough.
• Use your fingertips (they're the coolest parts of your hands) to work the dough and touch it as little as you possibly can.
• Refrigerating the dough regularly keeps it tender.
• Cooking the filling before it goes in the pie keeps the crust crisp and the apples juicy.
• Preheat the oven for 20 minutes before you bake the pie so the crust gets flaky.
• Check both the top and bottom crusts—when they're both golden brown, it's done. If the outside crust starts to brown too much before the rest is done, crimp strips of foil over the edges.
• Using a baking sheet both distributes heat evenly and catches drips of errant filling.
• Rotate your pie during baking for even browning.

slice apples

flute edge

Slip a metal spatula or dough scraper under the dough to keep it from sticking to the counter as you roll.

Fold the dough circle up into quarters, center the point in the middle of the pan, and unfold for hassle-free counter-to-plate action. Don't stretch the dough to fit the pan—if it's not big enough to fit, bring it back to the counter and roll it out a little more.

Always roll from the center out to the edge, rotating the dough a quarter turn each time to give you a large circle.

Add a little flour if the dough gets tacky. Go easy on the extra flour, though; too much will toughen the dough.

rolling wisdom

We like French rolling pins (the kind without handles) because they give you more flexibility.

birthday cake with chocolate frosting
serves 8 (8-inch layer cake) • prep time: 1 hour, plus 1 hour cooling time

Take the butter, eggs, and milk out of the fridge about an hour before making the cake so they can come to room temperature.

cake

	Oil for brushing the pans
2	cups cake flour or 1²/₃ cups all-purpose flour plus ¹/₃ cup corn starch
2	teaspoons baking powder
¹/₂	teaspoon fine salt
1¹/₂	cups plus 2 tablespoons sugar
¹/₂	teaspoon finely grated orange zest
1	cup (2 sticks) unsalted butter, room temperature
¹/₂	cup milk, room temperature
3	large eggs, room temperature
2	teaspoons pure vanilla extract

frosting

(Makes about 4 cups)

1¹/₄	pounds milk chocolate
12	ounces semisweet chocolate
2	cups sour cream (16-ounce container)
1	tablespoon coffee
1	tablespoon pure vanilla extract

Equipment: food processor, handheld electric mixer

1. To make the cake: Position a rack in the center of the oven and preheat to 350°F. Brush two 8-inch round cake pans with oil, line the bottoms with circles of parchment paper, lightly brush the paper and pan with oil, and dust with flour.
know-how 109

2. Put the flour, baking powder, and salt into the bowl of a food processor. Add the sugar and orange zest and pulse a few times to combine evenly. Cut the butter into small pieces and add to dry ingredients. Pulse until the mixture looks like coarse sand, with some pea-size bits of butter, about 5 times.
know-how 104, 107

3. Whisk the milk, eggs, and vanilla together in a liquid measuring cup. With the processor running, pour in the wet ingredients and process to make a smooth batter (this takes less than a minute). Divide the batter between the prepared pans and bake until a toothpick inserted in the center comes out clean, about 25 minutes.
know-how 107, 108

4. Cool the cakes on a rack for 15 minutes. Then run a knife around the edges of the pans, turn the cakes out onto a plate, and peel off the paper. Flip the cakes upright and cool completely on the rack, about 45 minutes. This is very important—icing a warm cake is not a happy thing.

5. Meanwhile, make the frosting: Break or chop chocolates into small pieces and put in a microwave-safe bowl. Microwave on medium for a minute, stir, and repeat until chocolate melts, about 3 minutes in all. Or put chocolates in a heatproof bowl set over an inch or so of water at a very slow simmer; set the bowl on the pan; don't let the bowl touch the water. Stir occasionally until smooth.
know-how 109

6. Let chocolate cool slightly, about 3 minutes. Stir the sour cream, coffee, and vanilla together; add to the chocolates. Beat with a handheld electric mixer until frosting is silky and fluffy. (Spread frosting soon after making it; it firms up at room temperature.)

7. Set a large flat plate on a large inverted bowl or bottom of a salad spinner (of course, if you have a cake stand, use that), dabbing a little frosting on the bottom of the plate to secure it. Place a cake layer top side up on the plate. With an offset or rubber spatula, scoop about one-third of the frosting onto the cake and spread it evenly to the edge of the cake. Place the other layer on top and press down

lightly. Spread another third of the frosting around the sides with a knife or offset spatula. Spread the remaining frosting on the top of the cake. Lightly touch the frosting with the back of a spoon to make swirly peaks. Serve immediately or set aside at room temperature for up to 2 hours before serving. If refrigerating the cake, bring to room temperature 30 minutes before serving.

make it your own

Use this batter to make 24 standard cupcakes. Fill paper-lined or buttered and floured cupcake pans ²/₃ full and bake for 20 to 25 minutes. Top with a half-batch of frosting.

cake wisdom

• Pulsing the dry ingredients gives you a lighter cake.
• Cakes bake best in the center of the oven.
• Don't open the oven too often; you lose up to 70°F each time.
• Press the center with your fingers to test doneness. If it bounces back, it's done; if it leaves a dent, keep baking.
• If the layers are uneven, use the thicker one on the bottom.
• This frosting keeps for a week in the fridge or a month in the freezer. Defrost in the refrigerator overnight or microwave gently until spreadable.
• When storing an already-cut cake, add half an apple to the cake box to keep the cake moist.

scoop on frosting

spread frosting

put second layer on

frost sides

smooth out

swirl top

cheesecake serves 8 to 10 • prep time: 2 hours plus 8 hours chilling time (inactive)

Take cream cheese and eggs out of refrigerator about 1 hour before making the cake.

crust

6   tablespoons unsalted butter
1½ cups graham cracker crumbs,
    or crushed chocolate wafers
    or shortbread cookies
2   tablespoons sugar
    Pinch fine salt

filling

2   pounds cream cheese,
    at room temperature
1¼ cups sugar
¾   cup sour cream
6   large eggs, at room
    temperature
1   tablespoon pure vanilla extract

1   teaspoon finely grated
    orange zest (see page 104)
1   teaspoon finely grated
    lemon zest (see page 104)

Equipment: 9-inch springform pan

for serving:

fresh berries (optional)

1. Position a rack in the middle of the oven and preheat to 325°F.

2. For the crust: Melt the butter, covered, in the microwave, or in a small saucepan over medium-low heat. Brush a 9-inch springform pan with some of the butter. Stir the remaining butter into the crumbs, along with the sugar and salt. Press the crumb mixture into the bottom of the pan, taking care to get the crust evenly into the edges. Bake until golden brown, 15 to 18 minutes. Cool. Wrap bottom and sides of pan with foil and put in a large roasting pan.

3. To make the filling: Beat the cream cheese on medium speed with a handheld mixer until smooth. Add the sugar and beat until light and fluffy, scraping the sides of the bowl and beaters as

needed. Beat in the sour cream, then beat in the eggs, vanilla, and orange and lemon zests just until combined; take care not to over-whip. Pour into the cooled crust.

▶ know-how 107, 108

4. Bring a medium saucepan or kettle of water to a boil. Set cheesecake in roasting pan, and carefully transfer pan to the oven (don't pull the rack out of the oven). Pour in enough hot water to come about halfway up the side of the pan. Bake the cheesecake for 1 hour—the outside of the cake will set but the center will still be loose. Turn the oven off and open the door briefly to let out some heat. Leave the cheesecake in the closed oven for 1 hour to finish cooking in the residual heat—this gentle finish minimizes the risk of cracking.

5. Remove cheesecake from the roasting pan to a cooling rack. Run a knife around the edges and cool cheesecake to room temperature. Cover and refrigerate 8 hours or overnight before serving.

6. Bring the cheesecake to room temperature 30 minutes before serving. Unlock and remove the springform ring. To serve, dip a knife in warm water and wipe dry before slicing each piece. Serve with berries, if desired.

cheesecake wisdom

Cooking cheesecakes in a water bath surrounds them with gentle, moist heat and wards off cracking. Turning off the heat when the center's still loose will give you a moister, creamier cake. Cracks aren't a big deal, though. A springform pan has sides that attach around the cake and can be easily removed, making it great for delicate, creamy cakes like cheesecake.

making a water bath

index

Look here for easy access to every recipe, ingredient, tip, and technique in this book.

Note: Recipe photographs are noted in colored numerals.

index

index

index

index

index

Food Network Kitchens has been teaching people how to cook for more than 10 years.

And viewers tell us that they still hunger for the absolute basics—for themselves, their kids, their mates.

So first thanks goes to our viewers' inspiration for our latest cookbook: *How to Boil Water*!

Very special thanks go to the brilliant Food Network Kitchens team who crafted the delicious recipes, tips, and lessons and styled these gorgeous photos.

Thanks go especially to Test Kitchen director (and former instructor) Katherine Alford and her team: recipe developer Mory Thomas, recipe testers Sarah Copeland and Suki Hertz, and assistants Tess Autrey Bosher and Mary Monahan.

Thanks also to culinary writer Rupa Bhattacharya; recipe editor Amy Stevenson; shoppers Dave Mechlowicz and Jacob Schiffman; food stylists, including coordinator Mory Thomas, Jay Brooks, Sarah Copeland, Santos Loo, and assistant Liz Tarpy; prop stylist Michelle Michaels; and photographers Robert Jacobs and Blaine Moats.

P.S. The faces in the book are all members of our Food Network Kitchens team, who wish you many fabulous homecooked meals that you will be proud to call your own.

—Susan Stockton,
VP Culinary Production

food
network

best selling
and award winning

Food Network Kitchens cookbooks provide for the ultimate culinary experience.

Find the inspiration and confidence to make every dish a success with fresh ideas, bold flavors and tips and techniques.

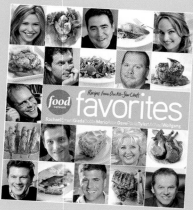

food network
favorites
Recipes from Our All-Star Chefs
Rachael Emeril Giada Bobby Mario Alton Dave Paula Tyler Michael Wolfgang

food network kitchens
making it
easy

food network
kitchens
cookbook
fresh ideas • bold flavors • tips & techniques

Taste the favorite flavors of some of the world's hottest celebrity chefs including Paula Deen, Giada De Laurentiis, Tyler Florence, Emeril Lagasse, Rachael Ray and more!

food network kitchens
get
grilling
Recipes, tips, and techniques for terrific food and big fun in the great outdoors

Available where cookbooks are sold and at foodnetwork.com

ADT0146_0406